Foundations of Modern School Practices

A Sourcebook of Educational Wisdom

Corey R. Lock

ROWMAN & LITTLEFIELD EDUCATION

A division of
ROWMAN & LITTLEFIELD PUBLISHERS, INC.
Lanham • Boulder • New York • Toronto • Plymouth, UK

Published by Rowman & Littlefield Education
A division of Rowman & Littlefield Publishers, Inc.
A wholly owned subsidiary of The Rowman & Littlefield Publishing Group, Inc.
4501 Forbes Boulevard, Suite 200, Lanham, Maryland 20706
http://www.rowmaneducation.com

Estover Road, Plymouth PL6 7PY, United Kingdom

Copyright © 2011 by Rowman & Littlefield Education

All rights reserved. No part of this book may be reproduced in any form or by any electronic or mechanical means, including information storage and retrieval systems, without written permission from the publisher, except by a reviewer who may quote passages in a review.

British Library Cataloguing in Publication Information Available

Library of Congress Cataloging-in-Publication Data

Library of Congress Cataloging-in-Publication Data Available
ISBN 978-1-60709-723-5 (cloth) — ISBN 978-1-60709-724-2 (paper)

Contents

Preface		v
Foreword		ix
Introduction		xiii
1	Administrators	1
2	Children	7
3	Classroom Management and Discipline	13
4	Classroom Practices	27
5	Curriculum	49
6	Education	57
7	Exceptional Children	69
8	Learning	75
9	Motivating Students	85
10	Parents	91
11	Schools	95
12	Students	113
13	Subject Matter	117
14	Teacher Preparation and Development	127
15	Teachers and Teaching	133
16	Teaching Methods	151
17	Testing	157
Epilogue		163

Sources 167
Index 173
About the Author 179

Preface

As a graduate student in the 1970s I began collecting old books about education. In time the collection grew to hundreds of volumes concerning every aspect of professional education. There were books about pedagogy, administration, philosophy, schools, testing and measurement, child development, teacher preparation, classroom management, education history, and countless other education subjects.

The great majority of the collection covered the 1840s to the 1950s. The interesting part of reading these books was discovering that many of the issues and concerns about schools and teaching written years ago still rang true for schools and teachers today.

I began sharing snippets and quotes from these early writings with my curriculum studies graduate students, and much to their amazement they discovered an "everything old is new again" refrain in the development of American education. What began as a sort of amusement with "then and now" comparisons of educational issues turned into a fairly serious pursuit of exploring the themes and messages that dominated the professional writings of the past.

It was not so much the history that fascinated students as it was the voices—voices that described schools, classrooms, and teachers with an uncanny familiarity. When students saw some of the things that were written about schools a hundred or more years ago they were amazed that practitioners are still coping with many of the same challenges faced by their professional predecessors.

This book contains hundreds of quotes and excerpts from the education literature of 1880 to 1935. These years were chosen because they were momentous, not only for the transformation of American education, they were pivotal years for the creation of a new era in America, an America of the twentieth century.

The nineteenth century ended with calls for social reforms to correct the excesses of the industrial revolution. Child labor laws were enacted, workers' unions were formed, and government began to look at the abuses of big business. Social reformers such as Jane Addams founded places for the unfortunate to live and schools took the responsibility of taking children from the factories and putting them in classrooms. America looked like it was going to become a big and important international leader with advances in transportation, communications, electronics, health care, and most significantly, education.

Between 1880 and 1935 the high school became the "people's college" and tried to recruit as many adolescents as possible. It was a time the child-study movement looked at childhood as a developmental period in life rather viewing children as small adults. Consequently kindergarten and elementary schools became places that nurtured rather than exploited children. Children with disabilities were brought into the schools and teachers were trained to teach the "unteachables."

The Efficiency Movement organized schools in ways that promoted uniformity and effective use of resources. Testing of the soldiers who were drafted during World War I revealed that the public schools had more work to do if its goal was to create a literate society. Some educators wanted to create a science of education and the development of dozens of standardized tests were used to measure every aspect of human development.

All these changes were written about in the books that were used to train and educate those who were to teach and administer the schools of the twentieth century. This book was produced to preserve some of those writings and share them with the educators of today. It was compiled to give modern education practitioners insights into their professional past. Sifting through this large body of literature of the past has revealed some wonderful insights into what the field of education was like in those early days.

Modern educators are often unaware that this rich and extensive body of literature exists, and that it explores a broad array of educational issues. They believe they need to develop new approaches to motivate students, manage classrooms, decide what is important to teach, find ways to make the curriculum relevant, engage students who would rather not be engaged, use tests to provide accurate information about student learning, and a wide variety of everyday, on-going issues that make schools battlegrounds of constant discord. However, these problems and concerns have been around for many years and much was written to describe what educators of the past did to address them.

Many of today's educators have not had the opportunity to explore the historical developments of their own profession. They often think the realities of teaching in today's schools require modern responses based in on-the-spot decision making. They might be surprised to learn that teachers in past could have so much to say about the kinds of problems found in modern classrooms.

We like to think that each successive generation of practitioners in all fields expand knowledge in ways that lead to new information that resolves difficult problems and issues. Medical practices in the twenty-first century have little resemblance to the practice of medicine in the early part of the twentieth century. The same can be said of communications, transportation, engineering, electronics, and most other professions. The pace of advancements in other fields cannot be said for educational practice.

In many ways American education has not evolved; it seems to keep reinventing itself. Many of the problems that frustrated teachers a hundred years ago continue to frustrate teachers today. The conditions that prevent teachers from being as effective as they would like to be have plagued teachers for generations.

THE SOURCES OF THE MATERIAL

The books that were used as sources were chosen at random from my collection. There was no attempt to create a particular line of persuasion, nor was there an attempt to find balance to counter points of view. The books are representative of typical training materials that were used in college and normal school educator preparation programs.

While the passages recorded here were taken from much larger pieces of writing, careful attention was given to insure that complex ideas were not reduced to simplistic sound bites, but rather, to capture the essence of important and interesting observations and arguments that were made for the creation of better schools. Care was taken to quote passages so that the selections retained the meaning and intent of the original works.

A WORD ABOUT STYLE

The modern reader may be a bit put off by the syntax and wording used by these early education writers. There was a sort of academic voice that appears stilted and awkward by today's standards; writers expressed themselves more elaborately (very wordy and embellished) than we would today.

Sentences were more complex than they needed to be and there were often misplaced modifiers. At times the writing became evangelical and the language would turn flowery and grandiloquent; for many educators, teaching was a calling much like the ministry and this belief was often reflected in the way they wrote.

Word choices are clearly early twentieth century. The children who are taught are invariably referred to as "pupils," only rarely as "students." "Percent," "meanwhile," "anyone," and "someone" were written as two words. Today and tomorrow were hyphenated as to-day and to-morrow. There are a number of words not found in common usage today such as audiles, developt, fetich, memoriter, practicalists, sloyd, tares, tragical, unfoldment, and visualizers. Spell and Grammar Checker often disapproved of how these early education writers expressed themselves. However, despite stylistic differences in writing, the meanings still come through clearly.

This is a book that can teach us a great deal about the history of education, but more than that, it is book I hope modern readers will enjoy.

Foreword

The period from 1880 to 1935 is generally thought of as encompassing the progressive era in America, including within education. This was a time of national urbanization and industrialization, a time characterized by the lives and careers of Harvey Firestone, John D. Rockefeller, Henry Ford, Thomas Edison and Albert Michelson, recipient of the first American Nobel prize in physics (1907).

The era begins with Social Darwinism and ends with Social Security. It is a time of war, of massive immigration, punctuated by the exclusionary acts of the early 1920s, of the rise of the Americanization movement, the "Red Scare," the execution of Sacco and Vanzetti, of marching suffragettes demanding citizenship rights, and, finally, of easy credit, soaring stocks, and the Great Depression.

For schools this was a period of organization and consolidation and for educators a period of rising professional aspirations that witnessed the emergence, standardization, and gradual strengthening of licensure requirements. Normal schools gave way to teachers' colleges which, in turn, morphed to become regional universities.

By the end of the period research and graduate study in education enjoyed a relatively prominent place on American college and university campuses even if much of this work, as John Dewey suggested, writing in *The Sources of a Science of Education* (1929), was thought of as being of dubious value: "That which can be measured is the specific, and that which is specific is that which can be isolated. The prestige of measurements in physical science should not be permitted to blind us to a fundamental issue: How far is education a matter of forming specific skills and acquiring special bodies of information which are capable of isolated treatment?" (pp. 64–65). Not much, was his conclusion.

Foundations of Modern School Practices: A Sourcebook of Educational Wisdom is composed of brief quotes from this period addressing a wide range of educational issues and concerns, many still current. That they remain current is not to say that how these issues and concerns are understood or addressed remains the same. Such a conclusion would be simply wrong.

Thank goodness few educators find I.Q. tests of any value today and that aggressive homogenous grouping is no longer often practiced. It is, however, to say that between birth and death human beings then as now continue to worry about how we are going to live together in a dangerous world, make a living, raise and enculturate children into some form or way of life, find and give others a little pleasure, make some sense of life's events, and somehow or another leave this world in a bit better shape than when we first encountered it. Learning occupies the space between birth and death.

The writers quoted in *Foundations of Modern School Practices: A Sourcebook of Educational Wisdom* represent a more or less random sample of education writers. I say "more or less" because the quotes are taken mostly from books collected by Corey Lock over a period of some forty years.

Not formally a random sample, these books survived most likely because they sold well. Outside of the occasional academic library, old textbooks in most fields generally end their lives in city dumps. The quotes give a glimpse into what was being discussed in normal school and college classrooms when teaching and school administration were the topics.

What is offered is mostly what would now be recognized as the *wisdom of practice*, spoken by generally well experienced practitioners who were thinking about, and sometimes studying, ways for making that practice more effective. Only rarely are the conclusions offered data driven, that is, outside of data that come from experience.

Ironically, for much of the past century practical experience has been denigrated in favor of rather abstract principles, generally produced by psychologists. Here it is worth noting that it was William James, America's most famous psychologist, in his *Talks to Teachers* (1899) who first warned educators about over-reliance for guidance from psychologists. His warning remains timely.

I had a lot of fun reading *Foundations of Modern School Practices: A Sourcebook of Educational Wisdom*. I have several favorite quotes, a few of which follow. Some made me laugh, others made me think: A. E. Winship writing on teacher supervision: "Teachers need inspiration rather than irritation. Teachers need leadership rather than authoritative direction,–more 'come' and less 'go'; more cheer and less fear" (1919). Amen!

"American children do not as a rule stand in awe of their parents, or really of their teachers, their ministers, or any one else in the community" (M. V. O'Shea, 1909). So: "Pile penalty upon penalty for misdemeanors, and let the '*sting*' of each penalty be double that of its predecessor" (William Chandler

Bagley writing on classroom management, 1911). Fortunately, not everyone agreed with Dr. Bagley's conclusion. Yet, "it is probable that both theory and practice are inclining toward the employment of other means than whipping to turn the young into paths of virtue, though distinguished teachers like President Hall still believe in the curative properties of 'Dr. Spankster's tonic'" (M. V. O'Shea, 1900). What does one do when the paddle breaks or the hand hurts? Professor Bagley suggested a "shingle may be profitably employed . . . although it should be noted that some authorities object to any blows upon the buttocks as unhygienic" (1911).

Olive Jones (1909) seems to have had her doubts about what we now call "best practice": "We are prone to think that in some one new method of teaching, or method of discipline, or method of classification and promotion, we have found a panacea for all the educational ills we have known." George Howland (1899) thought that if young people were educated, not merely trained, then education might be admitted into the august halls of the (not yet) respected professions: "When memory shall take its proper place and our pupils be taught to observe, to think, to do, instead of to memorize and repeat, then will the growth of our pupils compel the respect of the wise for our schools, and the fruit of the tree of knowledge be for the sustenance and health of the people." And finally, George Herbert Betts (1912) told his readers that the oft-made comparisons of education to law and medicine as models of practice was unwise: "it is impossible to test the validity of an educational theory as easily and satisfactorily as that of a medical theory or a theory of jurisprudence, the reason being that the results are so slow in education, and that there are so many supplemental factors to be taken into account."

There is much to enjoy and to ponder in *Foundations of Modern School Practices: A Sourcebook of Educational Wisdom*. As I read I thought of David Tyack and Larry Cuban's book, *Tinkering Toward Utopia* (1995). School improvement and educational change are often sources of considerable frustration among policy makers—who think things ought to change quickly and easily, a matter of legislating a new law–parents, no doubt children, and most certainly educators.

Change is mostly a human affair, not only a matter of altering behavior and thought but also of deeply embedded and institutionally supported relationships. If change could come easily and quickly to schools, I suspect that mostly the results would be harmful. But being satisfied with *tinkering* seems contrary to Western Enlightenment traditions, where the triumph of "good" ideas is expected.

As the quotes contained in *Foundations of Modern School Practices: A Sourcebook of Educational Wisdom* suggest, however, tinkering is what we do and mostly what we must do in education. Most of the authors quoted were, I think, thoughtful tinkerers. They sought to build an informed, lively, and powerful conversation about education that would encourage promising changes in behavior and understanding. This challenge remains with us today, and is perhaps more grimly insistent than ever.

Robert V. Bullough Jr.

Center for the Improvement of Teaching Education and Schooling (CITES), Brigham Young University

Introduction

You should understand
the way it was
back then, because it is the same
even now

—Leslie Silko, *Storyteller*

DEMOCRACY IN EDUCATION

This is a book of education ideas, commentaries, and observations from the past. The passages recorded here come from educational writings that were produced between 1880 and 1935, a time period that began with spirited calls for school reform and ended with a new and different concept of what it meant to be educated. It was this new concept of education that laid the foundation for the modern American school system.

The last two decades of the nineteenth century was a sort of fin de siècle for education. The approach of the twentieth century brought with it a great deal of discussion about school reform—discussion that would advocate a new kind of school designed for all the children of all the people.

Comprehensive education, once reserved for the wealthy who possessed sufficient leisure time for study, was now to welcome children from all sectors of society, the poor as well as the rich, rural and urban children, boys and girls, immigrants, minorities, and the handicapped. The schools were to provide comprehensive education from kindergarten through high school for children of all backgrounds. This new school that was "free, public, and universal" became known as "democracy in education."

Democracy in education was truly an American invention and writers often referred to it as the "great education experiment." At a time when there was mostly talk of school reform, Charles DeGarmo (1896) spoke of the coming reform movement as "a new era in education." Less than twenty years later, in 1914 Davenport said of the great education experiment:

> We are now engaged in the most stupendous educational, social and economic experiment the world has ever undertaken—the experiment of universal education; and whether in the end universal education shall prove a blessing or a curse to us will depend entirely upon our skill in handling the issues it has raised for our solution. We have entered too far upon this experiment ever to retire from it, even if we desired to do so, which we do not; and if the outcome is to be safety and not anarchy, and if it is all to result in further development of the race and not in retrogression, then a few fundamentals must soon be clearly recognized and brought into and made a part of our educational ideals, policies, and methods. (13–14)

This audacious idea that all children should receive a full and comprehensive education was promoted and articulated by John Dewey. With the support of many social progressives the schools began to teach children by embracing new concepts about child development, providing a curriculum that included practical knowledge along with the development of social skills, and using teaching methods that were humane and based in an understanding of how children learn. Traditional instruction that required students to memorize and recite with frequent testing was being challenged with more child centered approaches to teaching.

As democratic practices were adopted by the public schools, student enrollments exploded. Children who previously would not have had the opportunity to go to school were now encouraged to enroll.

The U.S. secretary of commerce provided yearly reports on school enrollments that documented the increases in student numbers. In 1880, 65 percent of five- to eighteen-year-olds were enrolled in public schools; by 1935, 83 percent of five- to eighteen-year-olds were in school. While this growth represented only an 18 percent increase in public school enrollments, the number of new students becomes very significant when the 1880 census, 50,155,783, is compared to the size of the population in 1935, 128,429,000 (U.S. Department of Commerce, 1940).

The growth in student enrollments was particularly dramatic in the public high schools. The public high school, sometimes called the "people's college" developed at a bustling pace. Krug (1969) reported, "At the beginning of the decade, in 1890, there were 202,963 pupils in 2,526 public high schools. By 1900 there were 519,251 pupils, and it took 6,005 public high schools to house them" (169). In 1935 the number of public high school students had multiplied more than tenfold to 5,669,156 who attended 23,614 public high schools (U.S. Department of Commerce, 1937).

Schooling in the 1880s largely took place in one-room schools where students were required to memorize and recite. The school term was short and irregular, often beginning sometime after Thanksgiving and lasting only three or four months. The teacher was the source of knowledge and his authority was not to be challenged.

Schools in rural areas often consisted of small log buildings, and in the cities classrooms were overcrowded with students who sometimes spent many hours working in factories before and after school. In both settings pupils in the same schoolroom could range in age from the very young to adults in their twenties.

However, as the twentieth century opened and developed, many of the new ideas promoted by education reformers took hold and by the 1920s schools looked completely different than they did some forty years before. The buildings were modern. They had kitchens, laboratories, gymnasia, lighting, and running water. The curriculum was much broader, schools were departmentalized, and teachers and administrators were professionally trained and licensed by their states (Wilson and Wilson, 1921).

By 1935 the schools were even more modern with administrators who had been "scientifically" prepared, teachers were mostly college graduates and many held graduate degrees, varieties of standardized tests were available to measure all aspects of student development, rural schools were largely consolidated and organized like schools in the cities, students were transported by motor busses, there were large extracurricular programs including organized athletic competitions, and college admission became the goal of many high school seniors.

These were the schools that evolved into education as we know it today. While the schools of 1935 are not the schools of today, they were far removed from the schools of the 1880s.

THE RISE OF EDUCATION LITERATURE

The dramatic changes that took place in education during this time period (1880–1935) were well documented in the education literature that grew as the schools adopted new concepts and practices. A great deal of writing about education was produced as reform changes took hold, and that writing increased at an astounding pace as America entered the twentieth century.

As early as the 1870s, D. Appleton, a publisher of school readers, created the International Education Series under the editorship of William Torrey Harris. This early work resulted in only a few education texts, namely Johonnot's *Principles and Practices of Teaching* and Bain's *Education as a Science*.

While most of the texts in the early years of this series were concerned with issues of educational philosophy and psychology, within less than twenty years Appleton published about 50 volumes in its International Series that related to practical issues of teaching and understanding the changes that were coming to the schools.

Between 1900 and 1935 an ever-growing expansion of educational writing formed a body of important philosophical, pedagogical, and administrative literature that guided the development of a modern education system. Hundreds of books on teaching, curriculum, school management, educational psychology, child development, philosophy, and other educational issues provided expert information to guide educators as they worked to create more inclusive and effective schools.

The major publishing houses (e.g., American Book, Macmillan, Charles Scribner and Sons, J. B. Lippincott, Row Peterson, Ginn, E. P. Dutton, Scott Foresman, and Bobbs Merrill) all formed departments to produce college textbooks for the rapidly growing field of educational pedagogy and other areas of educational practice.

At least a dozen publishers created special divisions to develop series of titles under the editorships of well-known educators. One of the more famous of these, Houghton Mifflin, launched the influential Riverside Textbooks in Education series under the editorship of Ellwood P. Cubberley in 1914.

The Riverside imprint produced more than one hundred titles related to educational pedagogy, and by the end of the 1930s had sold more than 3 million texts. Riverside also published a series of more than fifty Educational Monographs and a number of texts for teachers of vocational education. Throughout the 1910s, the 1920s, and the 1930s Riverside books were among the most used college texts for the training of school personnel.

In the 1890s there were but a handful of nationally distributed education journals. Education and school issues were written about in depth in many of the public commentary magazines of the day, but national periodicals solely devoted to education topics were scarce. By 1935 *Education Index* listed almost 150 specialized journals that dealt exclusively with education topics.

As the schools became more and more democratic, new challenges arose for administrators and teachers, and much of what was written in the books and professional journals between the years 1880 and 1935 describe school conditions, classroom practices, student behavior, parental support (or lack of it), curriculum development and a multitude of other school issues in ways that often sound very modern.

Introduction xvii

MAJOR THEMES AND TOPICS

More than 500 passages from more than 175 sources are recorded here. Major topics include: administrators, children, classroom management and discipline, classroom practices, curriculum, education, exceptional children, learning, motivating students, parents, schools, students, subject matter, teacher preparation and development, teachers, teaching methods, and testing.

If we were to look at old photographs from the 1880s to 1935 we would see what people looked like during those times. The clothing and mannerisms might look a bit strange, but we would see real people in real life settings. As we look into the world captured by the photographic records of the times, we would recognize a great deal of what life in the past was like. This is true for written records as well. Reading excerpts from the education literature of the 1880s to the 1930s is sort of like looking at photographs from another era. Instead of seeing differences in the clothing and mannerisms in photos we would find some strangeness in the word choices and syntax of the sentence structures. Yet, much of what was discussed in that literature continues to be discussed in the education literature of today.

There is a great deal in that writing that can inform us about the origins of our current practices. People in the past were not living in the past; they were living and working in their present and the things they wrote about were important to their everyday professional practices. This is a book of verbal photos that record how administrators, teachers, and other professionals were at work with the contemporary education issues and concerns of their day.

While there are references to practices and beliefs that we have thankfully moved away from, such as, strict obedience from students, the whipping post, the value of phrenology, and the use of hypnotic suggestion to control student behavior, modern readers who dip into this vast field of literature will marvel at how contemporary much of the writing sounds.

Much of the rhetoric in this professional literature is still with us today. For example, Hanus (1905) said that a trained teacher does not just teach subjects, but uses subject matter as a vehicle to change children. White (1886 and 1901) was concerned that an over-emphasis on testing had replaced teaching and he was critical of the amount of busy work teachers gave students. Parker (1883) believed that teachers were too closely supervised and they were not permitted to teach as they knew how. And, in 1899 Harriet Scott provided a fairly accurate description of constructivism. These, and many other examples of then and now issues, dominate these passages.

CALLS FOR SCHOOL REFORM

A constant and perennial theme in education has been the desire for change in the schools. Early education writers wrote of the need for school reform. They described inflexible and overburdened school curricula, phonics versus language usage methods to teach reading, college admission requirements that drove school programs, use of education lotteries to raise money for schools, repressive supervision of teachers, abusive testing practices, student apathy and disinterest in school, and a multitude of other educational concerns.

While the issues that need reforming appear to remain stable, the methods of the reform efforts to correct these conditions swing with vagary. The schools we know today are the result of earlier reform efforts.

Throughout the education literature of the late nineteenth century, all through the twentieth century, and into the twenty-first century there have constant calls for the reform of public education. As each generation of Americans demands reform of its public schools, what goes unrealized is that the conditions reformers want to be reformed are often the products of the last reform efforts, and that contemporary school changes will undoubtedly be overturned by the next generation of reformers.

In 1918, Charles Judd observed, "Every period doubtless seems to those who live and work in it to be more fruitful of reform than any preceding time in the world's history. Perhaps we exaggerate the extent and importance of the school reforms of the last twenty years, but they seem to be broad in scope and profound in meaning for the future" (71). Later he says of reformers, "There are some parents who are so enamored of the school which trained them that they are afraid of the new school which carries boys and girls along faster than pupils used to be carried through the elementary school. Such parents go back in imagination to the golden age of their childhood and fabricate notions about the excellence of those earlier schools which have no basis in fact" (71).

School reform efforts today have taken a somewhat dogmatic and powerful sweep through the states to organize the schools in more efficient ways so that student achievement can be measured in uniform and concrete ways. Beginning with *A Nation at Risk* and subsequently fueled by hundreds of state and blue ribbon panel reports, and the legislative requirements of No Child Left Behind, schools have become deeply invested in standard courses of study, frequent testing of students, close supervision of teachers often requiring that pacing guides and scripted lessons be closely followed, transforming the kindergarten from social and attitudinal activities to task and testing programs, and top down mandates from central office call for schools to fire teachers who cannot produce acceptable test results from their students.

In many ways, the schools of the late nineteenth century that needed reforming have become the schools reformers want to return to today.

While calls for school reform continue, the advice for teachers and administrators from this previous generation remains relevant. Teaching and administering schools is hard work. It was hard work in the past as it is hard work today. The passages cited here provide an opportunity for teachers of different time periods to communicate about the nature of that work.

Machiavelli, best known for those dark thoughts about political intrigue, said of the value of understanding past practices:

> Whoever wishes to foresee the future must consult the past; for human events ever resemble those of preceding times. This arises from the fact that they are produced by men who ever have been, and ever shall be, animated by the same passions, and thus they necessarily have the same results.

Machiavelli's observation appears to be particularly true for educators. The passages in this book demonstrate that past and present educators share many of the same concerns and passions about how to better educate children.

Chapter One

Administrators

As schools redefined themselves early in the twentieth century, new ideas about school administration began to emerge. The old model of the "principal teacher" and the traveling inspector was replaced by the university trained administrator who was academically prepared to properly manage the school. Administrators were no longer overseers who brought teachers in line; they were now school leaders who were trained to manage large comprehensive schools with efficiency and competence.

At the heart of this new administrative model was a belief in the abilities of teachers. Rather than directing teachers, the administrator's job was to remove the barriers that kept teachers from being effective in the classroom. Instead of directing the teacher, the principal was to listen, ask questions, guide, and suggest ways teachers could improve student performance. Largely through the efforts of Elwood Cubberley, a series of textbooks was developed to teach prospective school principals modern school management techniques.

The literature on school administration made it clear that board of education members often overstepped their authority by interfering with the operation of the schools. There were also admonitions to administrators who tried to micromanage the work of others. Interestingly, the average tenure of school superintendents today is about three-and-a-half years; Lewis reported that the tenure of superintendents in the 1920s was about the same as it is today.

ADMINISTRATORS

"The ideal administrator relieves those who do the actual teaching just as far as possible from tasks and worries that will distract them from their class work. He reduces their clerical labors to the lowest possible minimum . . . in order that both teachers and pupils may look upon the work of the classroom as the all-important business for which the school exists. But unhappily there are many supervisors and administrators who do not take this broad and stimulating view of their function. They load down their teachers with extra-scholastic duties and worries; they magnify the importance of clerical, administrative, and executive functions; they break into the regular routine for trivial reasons, and so undo much that the teacher has accomplished toward establishing a wholesome regimen of work. . . . Under conditions of this sort, the handicap of the teacher in keeping up an inspiring enthusiasm for his own work is greatly increased." —**William Chandler Bagley**, *School Discipline*, 1915, 125

AUTOCRATIC CONTROL OF TEACHERS

"Autocratic control of teachers is just as dangerous to the school as autocratic control of government is dangerous to the liberties of a people. It is out of harmony with the spirit of the age." —**Eugene Brooks**, *Education for Democracy*, 1919, 74

BOARDS OF EDUCATION

"The external management of the school is vested in the board of education, and the internal management belongs to the professional expert, the teacher. It is the office of the school board to furnish the necessary equipment and supplies, to appoint teachers and provide for their support, to make necessary regulations for the control of the school, and to sustain the teachers in the enforcement of discipline and in carrying out the work of the school. To the teachers belong the formulation of the course of study and its successful enforcement, the maintenance of discipline, the duty of instruction, and the direct furtherance of the educational purpose. This belongs to them because of their professional training and their expert knowledge. The function of the school will best be subserved when these relations between school boards and teachers are understood, and when they respectively fulfill the duties devolving upon them." —**Levi Seeley**, *Elementary Pedagogy*, 1906, 285–86

"The administration of the schools, the making of the course of study, the selection of texts, the prescription of methods of teaching, these are matters with which the people, or their representatives upon boards of education, cannot deal save with danger of becoming mere meddlers." —**John Dewey**, *Moral Principles in Education*, 1909, vii

CHIEF DUTY OF THE PRINCIPAL

"It is a chief duty of the principal to lead the teacher, in the performance of her detailed work in the class room, away from obsolete and inadequate standards toward rational thinking and high ideals. She must get away from any notion that education is merely a pouring-in and pumping-out process, or that recitation, important as it is, is the chief aim or sole activity of the school." —**Arthur C. Perry Jr.**, *The Management of a City School*, 1908, 207–8

MICROMANAGEMENT

"The superintendent may exercise necessarily detailed supervision. This usually implies that supervision of large problems is beyond his ability. If he is incapable of handling such matters as securing better school accommodations, raising the qualifications of teachers, attracting public opinion to the support of the schools, solving some of the perplexing modern educational problems, then must he fill in his time showing principals and teachers where to place the decimal point in a multiplication example." —**Arthur C. Perry Jr.**, *The Management of a City School*, 1908, 65–66

THE PRINCIPAL

"To many an earnest, enterprising principal, wholly devoted to the success and progress of his school, it doubtless sometimes occurs that if he were left free from the limitations of the course of study, unhampered by the rules of the board of education and without the annoying interferences from the superintendent's office, he could make a truly good school." —**George Howland**, *Practical Hints for Teachers of Public Schools*, 1899, 175

"In some schools, the appearance of the principal at the door [of the classroom] is the signal for the class to stand and recite some formula of greeting." —**Arthur C. Perry Jr.**, *Discipline as a School Problem*, 1915, 238

"The principal ought to be able to take a class from any teacher and teach it well, and he ought to know the details of school organization and the reasons for doing things in certain ways better than all except a few of his older and more capable teachers. In educational grasp, as shown by his ability to supervise and to give reasons for doing things, he ought to be distinctively the educational leader of the school." —**Elwood P. Cubberley**, *The Principal and his School*, 1923, 24

SCIENTIFIC MANAGEMENT

"Shortly after the success of scientific management in the commercial world was recognized, scientific investigators in the field of education began to transfer its terminology to the problems of educational management and direction. As a result, the scientific movement in education which is so fundamental to the new education, has been greatly stimulated and accelerated. As in the case of the factory, this movement attempts to define clearly the precise results which may be reasonably expected at every stage of the pupils' progress through the schools, to indicate the materials of instruction and the types of experience necessary to secure those results, and to determine the best types of organization and methods of work. The aim of scientific education is to secure the maximum results in all school work with the minimum expenditure of time, energy, and money." —**H. B. Wilson and G. M. Wilson**, *The Motivation of School Work*, 1921, 242

A SUPERINTENDENT'S ADVICE TO HIS PRINCIPALS

"[O]ne superintendent recently issued the following cautions, in printed form, to the principals of his city:
   MAY I REMIND YOU:

1. That the teachers are the real operators of the school plant.
2. That your chief function is to clear the way for them.
3. That their comfort, their self-respect, their potentiality, are to be safeguarded at every turn.

The wise principal not only guards but nourishes these three.

LET ME COUNSEL YOU:

1. To show respect unfailingly for the judgment and abilities of the teachers.
2. To judge them not too soon nor too late.
3. To hear their side through patiently.
4. To use the question five times to the declaration once.
5. To encourage every one in your corps to find her way of doing her job better.
6. To seek out unfulfilled capacity in both your teachers and yourself."

—**Elwood P. Cubberley**, *The Principal and His School*, 1923, 434

SUPERINTENDENT TURNOVER

"In 1923, Woody made a study of the tenure of the superintendents . . . in Michigan in their present positions (1921–1922). His findings are as follows: 'one-half of the superintendents in cities [with populations under 1,000] have occupied their present positions less than 1.4 years; one-fourth of them less than 0.6 of a year, and only one-fourth of them 2.5 years or more. In other words, three-fourths of them have been occupying their present positions not over two and one-half years. Stated in another way, if you should stand all of the 252 superintendents in a row according to the length of their tenure in their present positions and should start to count, beginning with the shortest tenure, you would have counted 100 of them before you came to the one who had occupied his present position three years. . . . [In] cities having a population of between 5,000 and 15,000, half of the superintendents have been occupying their present positions less than 3.5 years; one-fourth of them 2.1 years or less, and only one-fourth of them 8 or more years. It is significant that the tenure of superintendents in the larger cities is very little, greater than in the smaller cities.'" —**Ervin E. Lewis**, *Personnel Problems of the Teaching Staff*, 1925, 349

SUPERVISION

"Can the principal or superintendent convince the public that supervision is paying and that the expense is justified? In some counties the supervisors are important factors in the building and of the school and the community, while in others the people have declared war on them, and they have declared war on the people—a strange and unpardonable crime against humanity." — **Eugene C. Brooks**, *Education for Democracy*, 1919, 117

"Teachers need an entirely new line of advice and counsel. Teachers need inspiration rather than irritation. Teachers need leadership rather than authoritative direction; more 'come' and less 'go'; more cheer and less fear. There should be more drives for teachers and less driving of teachers." —**A. E. Winship**, *Danger Signals for Teachers*, 1919, vi

"Any teacher has a right to rebel against a supervisor who comes into his classroom merely for the sake of rating the work that he sees and leaving without suggesting the methods to be undertaken to improve the teaching that is being done. Criticism of this sort, which is purely negative, has been in many cases the cause of dissatisfaction upon the part of American teachers." —**George Strayer and N. L. Engelhardt**, *The Classroom Teacher at Work in American Schools*, 1920, 47–48

"The essential purpose of supervision is improvement of instruction." — **S. E. Davis**, *The Teacher's Relationships*, 1930, 142.

Chapter Two

Children

In this evolving educational system children were seen in a new light. Largely through the efforts of five influential child advocates—John Dewey, G. Stanley Hall, Arnold and Beatrice Gesell, and Nina Vanderwalker—childhood began to be viewed as an important period of human development.

Dewey promoted the idea that the whole child should be educated in schools. That is, children needed opportunities to develop physically, socially, and morally as well as intellectually. Dewey saw children as developing organically in all four dimensions of growth and that the school was to play an important role in all four areas of development. G. Stanley Hall, president of Clark University, was instrumental in forming the child study movement. He was the first to describe adolescence as a developmental stage of growth and he founded the *Pedagogical Seminary*, a journal that explored issues in child psychology.

In the early years of the twentieth century Arthur and Beatrice Gesell described norms in the developmental process during the first five years of growth. Some of these norms are still used by pediatricians today. Nina Vanderwalker promoted the value of preschool education and particularly the inclusion of kindergarten in the public schools.

Teachers were advised to consider each child as an individual and to be aware that children were at different stages of development. Children were not to be judged by particular behaviors but rather to be viewed in the context of their development.

THE CHILD

"The child is an organic whole, intellectually, socially, and morally, as well as physically. We must take the child as a member of society in the broadest sense, and demand for and from the schools whatever is necessary to enable the child intelligently to recognize all his social relations and take his part in sustaining them." —**John Dewey**, *Moral Principles in Education*, 1909, 8–9

CHILDREN

"Little children are delicate instruments, and they must be delicately handled, that their sensitiveness and possibilities may balance one another. Children are individualistic, personal, intimate; the teacher of children must enter into these experiences and imaginations of selfhood. She cannot deny children intimate contact if she would be of any service to them." —**Arnold Gesell and Beatrice Gesell**, *The Normal Child and Primary Education*, 1912, 245–46

CHILD–STUDY MOVEMENT

"The child-study movement has grown to be so complex that a notable effort was recently made to bring its many phases into closer relationship. In July 1909, there was held at Clark University a series of conferences which, in the light of the history we have sketched from prescientific times to the present, takes on considerable interest and significance. At these conferences were gathered leading representatives of the following interests: day nurseries, kindergartens, child psychology, medical education of defectives and subnormal children, open-air schools, tuberculosis in children, eugenic movements, psychological clinics, school nurses and physicians, settlement work for children, boy's clubs, Sunday school, industrial training, child labor, story-telling league, children's theater, playground movement, children's libraries, dancing and music, the juvenile court. It was a general child-welfare congress." —**Arnold Gesell and Beatrice Gesell**, *The Normal Child and Primary Education*, 1912, 27

CHILDREN TODAY

"'The young people of to-day, as compared with those of fifty years ago, are chiefly deficient in power of sustained attention and original thinking. They can not, or least, they usually do not, think as clearly, as patiently, and as cogently as did their fathers. They do not as quickly distinguish the irrelevant from the pertinent, the kernel from the husk, as the men of the last generation. They have an amazing fund of information; they are wide readers of bright, ephemeral literature; they have tasted every fruit on the great tree of knowledge; they know a thousand interesting scraps; they are more versatile and ingenious and attractive than any other of the recent generations. But they are quickly led astray by sophistry, and easily led to surrender conviction when it conflicts with interest.'" —**William H. P. Faunce**, president of Brown University, quoted by Thomas J. McEvoy in *The Science of Education*, 1911, 145

"From cradle to college we have been trying to make life, education, easy for the dear boys and girls. We have tried to please them ever and always, to keep them interested and amiable by trick and subterfuge, until we have built up a character that is satisfied only with that which gives it pleasure and gives it pleasure without any personal effort. As a result, will is weak and flabby, effort is purposeless, appetite is satiated, and life resolves itself into a dream of seeking for something easy and pleasant, and mentally is so weakened that resistance to overcome temptations or to surmount obstacles is almost impossible. The qualities that go to make up virile manhood or womanhood are possessed in but a negative degree, or are lacking altogether and strife upward and onward in intellectual and moral battles, the delight of robust manhood and womanhood, is only fitfully attempted, or is utterly refused. Is it any wonder that the army of incompetents, degenerates and criminals is growing?" —**Randall Saunders**, *The Teacher and the Times*, 1911, 80

THE CHILD WITH INITIATIVE

"Too often the child with initiative and individually is considered slow and troublesome, while the child that remembers and is able to give back the text or lecture is considered the satisfactory pupil. In this way the natural curiosity and inquisitiveness of the child is deadened in so far as school work is concerned." —**John William Hall and Alice Cynthia King Hall**, *The Question as a Factor in Teaching*, 1916, 165

MALADJUSTED CHILDREN

"The teacher of the primary grades has given into her care an extremely heterogeneous mixture of all sorts of adult maladjustments reflected in the children who have been in the care of these adults. She has spoiled little urchins who refuse to do anything unless constantly aided by their parents. She has contrary ones who do the opposite of everything that is wanted. She has those who have violent tempers and fly into a rage every time they are not satisfied with the course of events. She has sullen ones, pouty ones, priggish ones, mean ones, selfish ones, cruel ones, dishonest ones, as well as a few seemingly perfect angels. Such characteristics are commonly called person traits but the teacher must look upon them as symptoms; they tell her truly just where this particular child has made an error in his attempt to meet social conditions."—**John J. B. Morgan**, *The Psychology of the Unadjusted School Child*, 1930, 187

MISFIT CHILDREN

"There are no misfit children. There are misfit schools, misfit texts and studies, misfit dogmas and traditions of pedants and pedantry. There are misfit homes, misfit occupations and diversions. In fact, there are all kinds and conditions of misfit clothing for children, but—in the nature of things there can be no misfit children." —**Frederick Burke**, quoted by Adolf Meyer in *Suggestions of Modern Science Concerning Education*, 1917, 139; re-quoted by William Kilpatrick, *Source Book in the Philosophy of Education*, 1934, 451

NERVOUS CHILDREN

"Symptoms relating to intelligence are not as numerous or characteristic as the emotional and volitional symptoms. Nervous children are fully as likely to be bright as dull, but their intelligence is seldom of the most practical sort. The imagination is likely to be overactive. There is often an abnormal preoccupation with books, language, and abstractions as contrasted with things. These traits give the impression of mental precocity. The child is hailed as a prodigy, paraded as a genius, etc., with unfortunate consequences for his later development. Some of the wonder-children are stupid in everything except their exhibition specialties." —**Lewis Terman**, *The Hygiene of the School Child*, 1914, 295

THE PECULIAR CHILD

"The discovery of a defect in a child is no excuse for neglect of that child. The purpose of analysis is correction even if this takes additional time and energy. Remember that many of the most conspicuous successes in later life were very peculiar children in the classroom. *Pick out the peculiar individual and help him to make the most of himself.* Do not neglect him because he is peculiar for, in so doing, you may be overlooking the genius of the group."
—**John J. B. Morgan**, *The Psychology of the Unadjusted School Child*, 1930, 292

THE QUIET CHILD

"Do not be deceived into forgetting the quiet, good child. He may be the one who is most in need of your considerate attention." —**John J. B. Morgan**, *The Psychology of the Unadjusted School Child*, 1930, 135

Chapter Three

Classroom Management and Discipline

We sometimes think that schoolchildren were better behaved in earlier times. However, a great deal was written about classroom management and student discipline. Teachers were often judged more by how well they could manage unruly students than they were by their instructional skills.

Many writers counseled teachers to assert their authority in the classroom and that without good discipline proper instruction was not possible. Teachers were told that they should always maintain their own self control as they asserted their authority. They were also told that students had little respect for teachers who could not control their classrooms.

There was a lively debate about the value or the lack of value of corporal punishment, and some writers were sorry to see the end of a school tradition—the whipping post. Some thought that the demise of corporal punishment encouraged students to misbehave because misbehavior was a natural student response in the classroom. Educators bemoaned the negative attitudes school children had toward their elders and these negative attitudes were much worse than they had been in earlier times.

The child study writers believed that misconduct was often caused by the rigidity and inflexibility of the school and the classroom. Children who were kept busy with interesting and stimulating schoolwork did not have the time or inclination to misbehave. These writers asserted that the oversupervision of children and the lack of freedom in the school were the major causes of poor student behavior.

Modern practitioners might be surprised to learn that educators were concerned about drug problems and other antisocial behaviors among youth. Much of the writing about student conduct at the turn of the twentieth century will connect with today's teachers.

Chapter 3
ATHLETE MISCONDUCT

"When the [athletic] team consists of young men who are coarse in mind and language, or of boys who use cigarettes, strong drink, etc., or of those whose love for show is stronger than ambition to attain to the best ideals of school and life, or of boys who can easily be led to desecrate the Sabbath by public games, or of boys who think loudness of dress and manner is just the thing at home or on trips, the scholastic and moral possibilities of school athletics are quite disheartening. In such cases interest in practice and the prospective games associates those who should seldom be socially together, thus damaging nobler ambitions and character, and injuring the school that tolerates these things." —**Charles C. Boyer**, *Modern Methods for Teachers*, 1908, 78

ATTITUDES

"American children do not as a rule stand in awe of their parents, or really of their teachers, their ministers, or any one else in the community." —**M. V. O'Shea**, *Social Development and Education*, 1909, 334

"Let us face a very disagreeable fact. . . . The striking characteristic of the schoolboy is his attitude toward his work; an attitude of apathy, of unwillingness, and apparent inability to grapple with a difficulty. To the extent that would be alarming if we had not grown so accustomed to it, it may be said that the pupil does not care. He goes to school because he is sent; personally, too often he would prefer not to go. In school he does the things he is told to do. He does them sometimes well, often indifferently, sometimes badly." —**B. C. Gregory**, *Better Schools*, 1912, 41

AUTHORITY

"The authority of the teacher as sovereign in the school is in no way derived from, or dependent on the will of the pupil . . . nor is the teacher in any way amenable to the pupil for his mode of exercising it. So far as the pupil-subject is concerned, the teacher is, in the better sense of the term, a true autocrat, and may both take his stand and carry himself as such. . . . The teacher's authority as absolute must be imperative, rather than deliberative or demonstrative. His requirements and decisions, in whatever form presented, whether that of request, demand, or mandate, must be unargued. What he resolves upon and pronounces law, should be simply and steadily insisted upon as right *per se*, and should be promptly and fully accepted by the pupil as right, on the one ground that the teacher, as such, is governor." —**Frederick Jewell**, *School Government*, 1866, 50–54, quoted by William Kilpatrick in *Source Book in the Philosophy of Education*, 1934, 448–49

"There is . . . no exception to the principle that within the schoolroom the authority of the teacher is absolute. He may resent intrusion and interference with his work. He has legal support in evicting any visitor, even a parent, from the classroom. He has exclusive control and supervision over his pupils, subject only to such regulations and directions as may be prescribed by the trustees. He may make rules for the government of his pupils and may punish them for infractions of these rules. When we say that the teacher's authority is absolute, it is understood that the procedure of the teacher must be lawful and reasonable. Of course the criminal code to the relation of teacher and pupil; the teacher may not any more freely rob, assault, or murder his pupils in the classroom than in their homes. Nevertheless, his exercise of corporal punishment, is not in most States construed as assault." —**Arthur C. Perry Jr.**, *The Status of the Teacher*, 1912, 35–36

THE CHILD AT HOME AND IN CLASS

"The parent . . . says in all sincerity, 'My boy was reported for doing such and such; but I am sure he never did it; he never could have done it, for he does not behave like that at home.' True enough, he would not have done so had he been at home or if he had been receiving individualized instruction; but the parent does not know him, and would not recognize him, as a member of a crowd." —**Arthur C. Perry Jr.**, *Discipline as a School Problem*, 1915, 135

CLASSROOM MANAGEMENT

"Some teachers arouse all the combativeness in a child's nature by the tones or gestures employed in the slightest command. There is a 'Do this' which arouses every fiber in the boy to say, 'I won't!' There is a 'Do this' that causes him to bend every energy to the willing accomplishment of the teacher's purpose; there is still a third, which leaves him in utter indifference, and which might as well—yes, might better—have been left unsaid. The commands—rather, the words of the commands—are the same; the results are very different because the teachers' ways are different." —**Sarah Arnold**, *Waymarks for Teachers Showing Aims, Principles, and Plans of Everyday Teaching*, 1894, 238

"*[O]rder must be maintained at all hazards*, and if it cannot be done by the best method, then let it be done by an inferior one. It is better to appeal to motives which might be open to criticism from the highest ideal point of view than to attempt to teach *under conditions of disorder which offer no moral possibilities whatever*. Children have a wholesome contempt for people who come into a class-room and deliver gentle homilies on virtue, but lack the moral force to maintain order. Such teachers remind me of a missionary who proclaims peace and good will among cannibals *and is eaten up for his pains!*" —**Joseph S. Taylor**, *Art of Class Management and Discipline*, 1903, 46–47

"'What shall I do?' the young teacher will surely ask in this connection [classroom management]; 'What shall I do when I have tried every device that I can think of, and still fail?' There is no explicit formula that will cover each specific case, but one general suggestion may be given: *Get order*. Drop everything else, if necessary, until order is secured. Stretch your authority to the breaking point if you can do nothing else. Pile penalty upon penalty for misdemeanors, and let the '*sting*' of each penalty be double that of its predecessor. Tire out the recalcitrants if you can gain your end in no other way. Remember that your success in your life work depends upon your success in this one feature of that work more thoroughly than it depends upon anything else. You have the law back of you, you have intelligent public sentiment back of you. Or, if the law be slow and halting, and public sentiment other than intelligent, you have on your side right, justice, and the accumulated experience of generations of teachers." —**William Chandler Bagley**, *Classroom Management*, 1911, 96–97

"When a penalty has been promised, it should in every case be inflicted if the occasion arises. One of the worst habits in school mismanagement is to tell a pupil that he must accept a certain punishment for a misdemeanor and then 'back down' from inflicting that punishment. A 'suspended sentence' may sometimes be employed, but it is dangerous for the young teacher to practice this too often." —**William Chandler Bagley**, *Classroom Management*, 1911, 131

"It is safe to say that the majority of teachers go into their schools every September worrying more about one particular problem than all others combined; and this is the problem of government [management] in the classroom. Probably nine out of ten trustees and members of boards of education esteem *good order* more highly than anything else in teaching. In some communities the only school topic that is discussed is the order which the teacher keeps. He is regarded as a success just in the measure that he can make the children 'mind' or 'toe the mark.'" —**M. V. O'Shea**, *Everyday Problems of Teachers*, 1912, 1

"Children expect the teacher to control the school, and hold him in contempt if he does not." —**George Betts and Otis Hall**, *Better Rural Schools*, 1914, 183

"A cardinal rule of school management is to have few rules, and these very specific and relentlessly enforced." —**William Chandler Bagley**, *School Discipline*, 1915, 43

"Frequently, in a school of a single class, the logical method of dealing with the misconduct of an individual is to exclude him temporarily from the room. In a large school, however, it is necessary to prohibit the teachers from applying this method, because the thought might easily occur to three or four teachers along the same corridor at the same time, with the result that three or four pupils might be found picnicking in the hall." —**Arthur C. Perry Jr.**, *Discipline as a School Problem*, 1915, 206

"Professor Bagley has supplied the evidence that no classroom can be regarded as free from the appearance of unruly types of students. Even good teachers of long experience who in general are free from difficulties with the discipline of their classes find it necessary to give special attention to the troublesome types. These types are described by Professor Bagley as including the following: the stubborn pupil who makes difficulty because he is constantly refusing to fit into the social order; the haughty pupil who is not merely conceited but in his ordinary performances disturbs the regular social routine by his overbearing attitude both toward his fellows and his teacher; the self-complacent pupil who cannot be aroused to activity by any of the ordinary inducements that are presented by the school. Other types include the irresponsible pupil, the morose pupil, the hypersensitive pupil, the deceitful pupil, and the vicious pupil." —**Charles Judd**, *Introduction to the Scientific Study of Education*, 1918, 251

CORPORAL PUNISHMENT

"[I]t is probable that both theory and practice are inclining toward the employment of other means than whipping to turn the young into paths of virtue, though distinguished teachers like President Hall still believe in the curative properties of 'Dr. Spankster's tonic.'" —**M. V. O'Shea**, *Social Development and Education*, 1900, 347

"It is often argued that the knowledge that corporal punishment may be inflicted is enough to terrify the unruly, and so its use is seldom necessary. Experience proves, on the contrary, that the more severe and frequent is corporal punishment, the more hardened and reckless is the sinner who endures it. It is notorious that many of the most disorderly children in school are the very ones who are beaten most unmercifully at home. A rod in the hands of a teacher has no terror for such children. A kind word, a belief in your fairness and kindness and efficiency, will do far more than violence to reclaim these." —**Joseph S. Taylor**, *Art of Class Management and Discipline*, 1903, 64

"The theorists, who, appealing to popular prejudice, have succeeded in having corporal punishment legally prohibited in places, have not demonstrated that there has been a gain in moral development of pupils. The practicalists, who have the technical insight and experience, but not the popular side of the question, can readily demonstrate that in most cities the education of hundreds of pupils is thereby seriously hampered." —**Arthur C. Perry**, *The Management of a City School*, 1908, 281

"Many good teachers advise 'spanking' for young children, and there is much to recommend this traditional means of discipline. Upon those who have grown callous to the palm of the hand, a shingle may be profitably employed, although it should be noted that some authorities object to any blows upon the buttocks as unhygienic—maintaining that they tend to cause congestion of the capillaries in the neighborhood of the genital organs, thereby giving rise to serious dangers." —**William Chandler Bagley**, *Classroom Management*, 1911, 127

"The total abolition of corporal punishment, under a sickly sentimentalism that will soon be weeping over the fading of a flower, is leaving young and irresponsible lives to a license that breeds contempt for authority, and that encourages unrestrained gratification of every evil passion; and boards of education and parents who do not, at least, grant the wisdom of the power to exercise that reasonably forceful restraint sanctioned by the Penal Code of New York state, are sowing to a wind that will certainly be reaped as a whirlwind of riotous license and irreclaimable abandon." —**Randall Saunders**, *The Teacher and the Times*, 1911, 81

"With some very severe cases which do not easily yield to treatment, it is necessary to resort to corporal punishment. The younger a child, the more effective is physical pain. As he grows older, mental and spiritual penalties grow increasingly effective. A whipping means little to the sixth-grade boy; the pain is due rather to the humiliation which comes with the punishment. If a teacher is able to make a pupil appreciate the evils of his conduct by using other than physical penalties, he should, of course, do so; but when all other plans fail, corporal punishment is justifiable, since obedience and respect for social law must be learned sometime during a lifetime." —**W. W. Charters**, *The Teaching of Ideals*, 1928, 233–34

DEPORTMENT

"A recent investigation in a public school disclosed the fact that money furnished by parents for school material, as they supposed, had been used by a number of the boys to buy cigarettes." —**Emerson White**, *School Management*, 1893, 98

"The conduct of boys and girls on the school grounds and in the halls of the school building, where they are under less restraint than in the schoolroom, is a test of their gentlemanly and ladylike character. It is not a universal custom, even in representative colleges, for students to remove their hats on entering the halls. This is customary, however, in many colleges and schools, and is to be encouraged, as an act of gentlemanly propriety. A sense of delicacy will lead boys to precede girls in ascending stairways, and to give them the precedence in descending. Boisterousness in the halls is inadmissible, whether within or without the hours of the school session. Where gentlemanly and ladylike instincts prevail in the pupil, they will not fail to manifest themselves at all times and places." —**Robert King**, *School Interests and Duties*, 1894, 198

"Among students, almost from the primary grade up, there is a sort of tradition that it is not only not wrong, but rather the correct thing, to take what advantage they can of the teacher, and cheat him into a good opinion of their ability; and pupils do this who would scorn to lie or cheat on the playground or in their social relations." —**Ruric Roark**, *Psychology in Education*, 1895, 234

"An abscess is not a pretty thing: neither is a boy who tells his teacher to go to hell." —**Arthur C. Perry Jr.**, *Discipline as a School Problem*, 1915, 6

"Shall pupils be permitted to whisper, write notes, leave seats without permission, play marbles 'for keeps,' loiter on the playground after the signal has been given for assembling or dismissal, throw snowballs, run down stairways, play boisterously in the classrooms, chew gum, choose their own seats at the beginning of the term, correct each other's papers? Relative to these and a host of other specific situations of school economy, concerning which inexperienced or mechanical teachers are ever asking, 'What would you do if—?' there can be no universal answer." —**S. E. Davis**, *The Work of the Teacher*, 1918, 105

DISCIPLINE

"But whenever you *do* command, command with decision and consistency. If the case is one which really cannot be otherwise dealt with, then issue your fiat, and having issued it, never afterward swerve from it. Consider well beforehand what you are going to do; weigh all the consequences; think whether your firmness of purpose will be sufficient; and then, if you finally make the law, enforce it uniformly at whatever cost. Let your penalties be like the penalties inflicted by inanimate nature—inevitable." —**Herbert Spencer**, *Education: Intellectual, Moral, and Physical*, 1860, 226–27

"Extremely difficult though discipline be, one thing should be perfectly clear in the teacher's mind, viz., the aim of discipline. Many teachers regard discipline as a series of defensive acts, designed to keep children from tearing down the school-house or from infringing upon one another's rights. To such teachers the aim of discipline is 'to keep order.' But order is simply a means to an end. Conformity to the law of things is desirable, but the spirit of conformity means the right attitude toward things while conformity does not include this element. The orderly coming into the schoolroom is most valuable when it is done without pressure or penalties. The fundamental aim of discipline may then be framed as we phrase the aim of education, viz., *the development of the child into an efficient, ethical, social being*." —**John Alexander Hull Keith**, *Elementary Education: Its Problems and Processes*, 1905, 87–88

"There are two kinds of teachers as regards school discipline. One teacher keeps the children under a severe restraint by a spiritual power which I compare to the power of the hypnotizer. I have seen teachers who could hypnotize, as it were, the children into a vivid consciousness of the teacher's will, subordinating their own likes and dislikes to the teacher, sometimes in dread of the teacher's power and sometimes out of awe and respect or even affection for the personality of the teacher. I do not consider the discipline of such teachers to be a health-giving effect in a school. I prefer the other kind of teacher who does not tyrannize, so to speak, over the child's mind either by fear or by affection and does not insist on the self-effacement of the child in the presence of the school. The teacher should encourage step self-activity on the part of the pupil, but he should not go so far as to undertake to make the child assume dramatically the role of free citizen, for this is to learn to play a part, conforming one's self to an external model as an ideal." —**William Torrey Harris**, *The City School*, 1906, 13–15

"Do not, then, for mere sake of discipline, command attention from your pupils in thundering tones. Do not too often beg it from them as a favor, nor claim it as a right, nor try habitually to excite it by preaching the importance of the subject. . . . Elicit interest from within, by the warmth with which you care for the topic yourself." —**William James**, *Talks to Teachers*, 1910, 111

"Good discipline comes rarely as the result of much talking. The teacher whose words fall with the incessant patter of rain-drops will soon find the children with their umbrellas of indifference raised for protection." —**Florence Milner**, *The Teacher*, 1912, 134

"A teacher with a sense of humor can solve many difficult problems in discipline, where a teacher without it would fail altogether. The errors of the school-room, in respect alike to intellectual work and to conduct, may often be best corrected if the teacher will take a humorous rather than a tragical view of them. . . . Conflict is often rendered more intense by solemn, sedate, angry attitudes in the teacher. Humor releases nervous tension, brings into action the better feelings, and causes one to take a more joyous view of things." —**M. V. O'Shea**, *Everyday Problems of Teachers*, 1912, 305–6

"The very fact that the pupil so often is lawless, destructive, rude and noisy as soon as restraint is removed proves, according to the advocates of 'discipline' by authority, that this is the only way of dealing with the child, since without such restraint the child would behave all day long as he does when it is removed for a few uncertain minutes." —**John and Evelyn Dewey**, *Schools of To-morrow*, 1915, 134

"It has been recognized by teachers for many years that if pupils are kept busy with interesting, educative tasks, there will be few disciplinary problems." —**Charles Holley**, *The Teacher's Technique*, 1924, 25

DISCIPLINE THROUGH KNOWLEDGE

"However much the ultimate theories of education may differ, it may fairly be asserted that in elementary education our best thinkers unite in the opinion that concrete, interesting matter is far preferable to the dry bones of purely formal and mechanical instruction. In place of the old motto of discipline *and* knowledge, we have really adopted in practice the new one, viz. discipline *through* knowledge." —**Charles DeGarmo**, *Herbart and the Herbartians*, 1895, 244

DISOBEDIENCE

"The formality of the average classroom encourages disobedience. The teacher who overburdens the children with rules and regulations invites rebellion. A natural impulse toward order is frequently inhibited by too much prescription. Some well-meaning teachers, by too much negative suggestion, call out a new list of juvenile offenses every day. There is a stain of perversity in human nature which, if provoked, swells into obstinacy and armed resistance. Beware that you have your class with you and not against you, for children catch the mood of their companions and are very versatile in their ways of signifying it." —**Arnold Gesell and Beatrice Gesell**, *The Normal Child and Primary Education*, 1912, 253

Chapter 3
DON'T SMILE UNTIL CHRISTMAS

"In the case of a young teacher it will usually be safer at first to be a little too strict rather than too lenient." —**Edwin Kirkpatrick**, *Fundamentals of Child Study*, 1916, 348–49

DRUGS

"Heroin—'scat' or 'joy powder' in the vocabulary of its devotees—forms a fixed habit very quickly, and one that is practically incurable. In some schools the habit of inhaling chloroform becomes a fad before the teachers are aware that it has been introduced. In one small town of the Middle West a boy had formed an incurable habit, which so interfered with his work that he was finally compelled to leave school, before his teachers had any inkling of the cause of his sleepiness and dullness. Children who lay their heads upon the desk, with handkerchiefs over their faces or with hands covering the nostrils, should be watched carefully. In large cities it is not uncommon to find children addicted to cocaine, which can be used in ways that defy detection except to experienced observers. The use of headache powders of various sorts, especially those based upon phenacetin and acetanilide, widely advertised under pseudo-medical trade-names, should be guarded against carefully. Many high school girls form the habit of dependence upon such compounds without understanding the danger of their use." —**Frances Morehouse**, *The Discipline of the School*, 1914, 158–59

"There are two opposing points of view, one contending that any publicity particularly instruction of the adolescent, will have the adverse effect of increasing rather than diminishing the use of drugs and the number of drug addicts, and the second maintaining that a well-planned educational policy, carried out in the schools, will result in a marked decrease in the drug habit."
—**E. George Payne and J. L. Archer**, "Narcotics and Education," *The Journal of Educational Sociology* 4 (February 1931): 370

HYPNOTISM AND EDUCATION

"In this connection, I will briefly refer to the work of Dr. Quackenbos of New York, who has been successful in treating, among others, deficient pupils by post-hypnotic suggestions. Those in whom habit has destroyed will-power seem to need the stimulus of another will for their self-recovery through right action. The cases that have shown themselves amenable to such treatment include alcoholism, social vice, cigarettes, drug habits, kleptomania, bad temper, cruelty, habitual falsehood, and loss of interest in study and books. The use of both waking and hypnotic suggestion by modern reputable physicians in dealing with sick patients dignifies this method as of possible service to the teacher in dealing with sick minds." —**Herman Harrell Horne**, *The Psychological Principles of Education*, 1909, 290

MAINTAINING ORDER

"The arrangement of seats in the school-room, and more particularly for recitation purposes, should be such that all pupils may be easily observed by the teacher without special effort. Watching for disorder or inattention is disagreeable and irksome to an instructor and offensive to all well-disposed pupils." —**Daniel Putnam**, *A Manual of Pedagogics*, 1899, 205

"Methods of discipline may be as mechanical as are methods of instruction. Pupils may be arranged in their seats in such order as to please the eye of a spectator. The position of each pupil in his seat may be in form and uniform. Each sits, turns, rises, moves, just as he is required to do. Sometimes even the lock-step used in prison discipline is required, so that no pupil may get out of order in ranks. At study, the eye must be kept at a uniform distance from the book, no matter what the condition of the eye. Regularity of movement is desirable." —**J. L. Picard**, *School Supervision*, 1905, 131

OFFICE REFERRALS

"Never in haste or in anger should a pupil be referred to the office, and, save in the rarest of cases, not till the principal has been seen by the teacher and fully informed of the nature of the fault or failure. Often this conference itself will render it unnecessary to send the pupil at all." —**George Howland**, *Practical Hints for the Teachers of Public Schools*, 1899, 157

PUNISHMENT

"[W]e must be content with urging that modes of punishment be so regulated as to interfere to the smallest extent with teaching. If the offender is punished by a tedious exhortation, the whole class is punished, and bored, at the same time. If the offender is to be disgraced by being made to stand apart, let him stand at the back of the room, where he will be out of sight of all except the teacher. But if it is necessary to exclude him repeatedly from the class, the question soon arises whether he ought to be retained there at all; for a pupil who attends school merely to be 'kept out of mischief' can be better kept away from school." —**J. J. Findlay**, *Principles of Class Teaching,* 1911, 391

RESPONSIBILITY

"Encourage children to take the just blame for what they do rather than to make excuses which transfer the blame unfairly to accidents, false causes, or to other individuals." —**John J. B. Morgan**, *The Psychology of the Unadjusted School Child,* 1930, 185

SCOLDING

"The scolding teacher is often the bad boy's sweetest opportunity, for he can always contrive to answer back, a chance he dearly loves and persistently labors for." —**George Howland**, *Practical Hints for the Teachers of the Public Schools,* 1899, 109

"What a doleful mistake it is to scold individual pupils in the presence of the whole class! At such times a teacher too often exceeds justice, and speaks bitter words which leave a sting behind difficult to be effaced. As far as possible all serious breaches of conduct on the part of individual pupils are to be treated privately, when by tact and skill the teacher will win the pupil's confidence, and make him his strong and ardent ally." —**Samuel Dutton**, *School Management,* 1903, 88–89

SELF-CONTROL

"Govern yourself; do not get angry. Never let pupils see that you are annoyed. Nothing so delights mischievous or vicious pupils so much as to see that they can annoy the teacher, and they are quick to follow up an advantage thus gained. Woe to the teacher who thus places herself at the mercy of 'young tyrants!'" —**J. M. Greenwood**, *Principles of Education Practically Applied,* 1901, 59

"It is desirable, therefore, that the teacher have self-control developed to a remarkable degree. Schoolroom situations frequently have such a degree of intensity as to excite strong emotions. The teacher who yields to these sudden tides of feeling not only sets objectionable copy for the pupils, but also lowers himself in their estimation. Aside from reasons just given, every teacher needs self-control for the sake of saving his own power and vitality. And, finally, leaving all low utilities out of account, self control is worth while just for its reflex influence on one's character." —**J. A. H. Keith**, *Elementary Education: Its Problems and Processes*, 1905, 108

"When I taught school, there were many times when the indifference, stupidity, flippancy, or silliness of the class brought me to such a pitch of rage, that I dared not trust myself to speak. I would clutch the arms of my chair, and swallow foam until I felt complete self-command; then I would speak with quiet gravity. The boys all saw what was the matter with me, and learned something not in the book." —**William Lyon Phelps**, *Teaching in School and College*, 1912, 23

SUPERVISION OF CHILDREN

"A child who is watched and controlled every moment of the day has no opportunity to develop the power of self-direction. Hence the teacher must get rid of the watching habit. He is no detective; and he must not treat the child as if he were a thief. Pupils must understand that it is dishonorable to misbehave in the absence of the teacher. Classes can be so trained that they may be left alone without danger of disturbance. Even 'bad' children like to be trusted. If you find it necessary to leave the room, say: 'Shall I appoint a monitor to watch you, or would you rather take care of yourselves?' Children will always prefer the latter course. Make it a rule that the one time of all times when the class and the individual must be models of propriety is when the teacher's back is turned or when he is out of the room." —**Joseph S. Taylor**, *Art of Class Management and Discipline*, 1903, 36–37

TARDINESS

"For the habitually tardy pupil there is probably no remedy so effective in stimulating time judgment as a judicious use of corporal punishment, provided, of course, that the tardiness is due entirely to the pupil's carelessness."
—**William Chandler Bagley**, *Classroom Management*, 1911, 78

WHAT AILS THE YOUTH OF TODAY?

"What ails the youth of today? Every one is ready with an answer. 'They have grown perverse because we have ceased to administer the old-fashioned discipline,' says one. . . . The faults of youth are due less to relaxation of the old discipline than to the inadequacy and illusoriness of it." —**George Coe**, *What Ails Our Youth?* 1924, vii–ix, quoted by William Kilpatrick in *Source Book in the Philosophy of Education*, 1934, 478

THE WHIPPING POST

"Think of yourselves at the call and beck of the parent who could take his little boy or girl up to the public whipping-post to be flogged by a hired baster, and him or her to be found in the free school, and there intrusted with the tenderest and most delicate interests of life! Believe me, my fellow teachers, our schools will be mentioned with scorn and our names spoken with contempt till we cast aside this relic of a by-gone age, and cease to be the sole representatives of a debased and degrading barbarism." —**George Howland**, *Practical Hints for the Teachers of Public Schools*, 1899, 30–31

"If [the superintendent] discourages the use of the rod, he will find more objectionable instruments of bodily harm. If he permits and advises the use of the rod, it will be wielded too vigorously, and with no beneficial results. If he enjoins upon some special teacher the exercise of this right for the whole school, the whipping-post will be firmly planted and frequently used." —**J. L. Picard**, *School Supervision*, 1905, 133

Chapter Four

Classroom Practices

A great deal of advice about classroom practices, understanding the learner, and teaching effectiveness became part of the pedagogical literature of the late nineteenth and early twentieth centuries. The old teaching practice of having students read, memorize, and recite changed to more student friendly instructional methods.

Students were to take a more active role in their own achievement as the teacher structured classrooms that encouraged student learning. Teachers came to understand that children developed and learned at different rates. The teacher learned to diagnose where children were and then helped them to develop into productive citizens.

The pedagogy for teachers discussed such issues as lesson planning, the value of homework (an argument that continues today), questioning skills, grouping, and a wide range of ways to stimulate student thinking. Teachers were told to eliminate busy work and to give students opportunities to become independent learners. It is interesting to note that teachers were told to use the first day of school to establish a culture for learning that would set the tone for the rest of the year.

Teaching was seen as serious work and there was talk of it becoming a profession.

BEHAVIORAL OBJECTIVES

"Almost every objective of education can be stated as the ability to do something, whether subjective or objective. The principle above stated therefore applies to practically the whole of education." —**Franklin Bobbitt**, *How to Make a Curriculum*, 1924, 51

BUSY WORK

"Too often the teacher's chief purpose in assigning the busy work is to keep the child quiet until the period of his next recitation." —**Sarah Arnold**, *Waymarks for Teachers Showing Aims, Principles, and Plans of Everyday Teaching*, 1894, 218

"There is one other use of written work that needs only to be mentioned to be condemned. We refer to the assigning of pencil and pen work, *to keep pupils busy*, a practice less common, it is hoped, than it was a few years ago. It is, of course, admitted that the keeping of pupils busy is an important condition in the easy government of a school, but no competent teacher is obliged to impose work *for this special purpose*." —**Emerson E. White**, *The Art of Teaching: A Manual*, 1901, 104

CRITICAL THINKING

"Among the many problems of the teacher, it appears that an outstanding one is that of developing critical thinking habits. Critical is used here in the sense of meaning analysis, reflection, and judgment in a given situation. It cannot be easily refuted that this type of activity, namely critical thinking, is the most strenuous of all human behavior. Perhaps this explains the prevailing lack of it among people in general." —**Ned Dearborn**, *An Introduction to Teaching*, 1925, 71

CULTIVATION OF THE INTELLECT

"Even in his own special domain, the cultivation of the intellect, the teacher is not absolute. He cannot make poor soil rich; he cannot (if he would) keep others from working the same field; and he cannot (though he would) prevent the enemy from sowing tares." —**David Salmon**, *The Art of Teaching*, 1903, 2

ESTABLISHING CLASSROOM ROUTINES

"Pupils should be taught to begin work promptly by specific instructions and daily practice in such matters as laying out materials, forming a clear idea of the results to be reached, and planning the work of the period. Routines should be devised for the preparation, distribution, and collection of supplies and materials. The larger the pupil's responsibility for the routine, the better." —**Douglas Waples**, *Problems in Classroom Method*, 1929, 365

FIRST DAY OF SCHOOL

"The first day should leave with the pupils a distinct impression that work has begun in earnest, that no time has been 'frittered away,' and that something definite has been accomplished." —**William Chandler Bagley**, *Classroom Management*, 1911, 29

"The teacher must come to the first day . . . with as full information as possible of the problems to be met, and with plans carefully matured for the organization and management of the school. The first day must be a success. Nothing must be left to chance. The teacher must show no indecision, hesitancy or doubt in forming the classes, assigning the work, initiating the program, or doing any of the many other things necessary in starting the school. He must be fully in command of the situation from the first moment, and neither falter nor blunder." —**George Betts and Otis Hall**, *Better Rural Schools*, 1914, 167–68

FLASH CARDS

"If one must memorize vocabularies the best method is to prepare small slips of paper. On one side write the English term and on the other side the foreign equivalent. In studying the vocabulary pick up the slip of paper, read off the term on one side and recall its equivalent. If this cannot be done, turn the paper over and repeat the two terms several times together. After thus going through the list, shuffle the slips of paper and repeat the process." —**Edward Long Jr.**, *Introductory Psychology for Teachers*, 1922, 82

GROUPING

"In New York City schools have tried several experiments to meet the needs of the exceptional child, not meaning thereby the mentally defective. One of these, an interesting account of which appeared in the *Educational Review* of June 1898, provides that each grade shall be divided into classes for slow and bright pupils. The same idea was extended a little further in another school, where the plan entails three divisions: one, the bright children of the grade;

second, the slow pupils of the same grade; and third, the over-age children of the two grades in the same year. In both these schemes the divisions progress at a different rate of progress, the brighter child doing more extensive and intensive work on the same subject-matter, and both plans allow the children to pass from one division to another at the end of a term, according to the differences in development of their mental capacity." —**Olive Jones**, *Teaching Children to Study*, 1909, 7

"There are schools where certain classes are avowedly named as for blockheads, and the members of it reckoned as a disgrace to the community: such a scandal should be impossible. But it is no discredit to a school to sort out its pupils according to their needs, in a spirit, not of contempt, but of consideration for the talents and needs of all alike." —**J. J. Findlay**, *Principles of Class Teaching*, 1911, 400–1

"Various devices have been suggested for the treatment of the supernormal. In general, the principles underlying these suggestions are the same as the principles for the treatment of subnormals. Separate the unusually bright and give them a type of training which will best develop their personal powers." —**Charles Judd**, *Introduction to the Scientific Study of Education*, 1918, 175

"There has always been a tendency for schools to recognize and care for, often unkindly, pupils who are dull or for other reasons backward. Teachers have given such pupils a relatively inordinate amount of time in class and have kept them in after school, and in one high school visited there was what was popularly called a 'bonehead room' to which was assigned pupils who had fallen behind in their work! The plan of homogenous grouping provides that the bright be recognized as well as the dull, that each group be taught according to need, and that it shall progress at its optimum pace. That there are wide ranges of natural ability, all stages of which should receive special and appropriate attention, may be seen in the reports of the achievements of pupils when measured by the Army Alpha Tests." —**Thomas Briggs**, *The Junior High School*, 1920, 147

HIGH EXPECTATIONS

"The amount of moral injury which results from constantly demanding less of children than they are capable of doing, and from keeping them on work that has grown stale to them, cannot be estimated." —**George Edmund Myers**, "Moral Training in the School: A Comparative Study," *Pedagogical Seminary* XIII (December 1906): 448

"The teacher who does not insist on absolute accuracy in the work of her pupils,–who does not make clear and plain every process in the work, and who does not insist on and secure so far as possible perfect preparation for recitation and perfect recitations, is doing incalculable harm to her pupils, and should not be surprised if her pupils are evasive, evasive, shiftless and disorderly—absolutely without honor." —**Randall Saunders**, *The Teacher and the Times*, 1911, 55

"A . . . requirement of the good answer is that it shall be matured. The teacher who accepts an answer which does not represent the student's best thought is encouraging careless thinking. In contrast to a common attitude among students that the answer is merely to satisfy the teacher, and that whatever thus satisfies is all that is called for, the student must be led to take his answer seriously. The teacher should develop the student's self-criticism, so that he will be dissatisfied with any effort which does not represent him at his best." —**Herbert Foster**, *Principles of Teaching in Secondary Education*, 1921, 68–69

HIGH STANDARDS

"Merely presenting high standards to children acts as a suggestion for their acceptance; that is, in a school where standards are high, the children more or less unconsciously come to believe in these standards and to accept them as being right. The teacher may and will talk about them and particularly will expect them to be followed. It is therefore natural that the child should be inclined and induced to accept them." —**W. W Charters**, *The Teaching of Ideals*, 1928, 251–52

HOMEWORK

"The parent has been annoyed too often by the doctrine that the home is responsible for the teacher's work." —**Preston Search**, *An Ideal School or, Looking Forward*, 1902, 109

"Little study should be required of pupils in the elementary grades outside of school—none whatever before seventh school year, and not to exceed three-fourths of an hour daily for that year; for the eighth school year, not to exceed one hour." —**Edward Shaw**, *School Hygiene*, 1910, 233

"When once prescribed, the [home] work must be 'exacted,' *i.e.,* it must be heard, examined, corrected, as early as possible on the following day, and marks assigned for it; penalties imposed for gross neglect." —**J. J Findlay**, *Principles of Class Teaching*, 1911, 407

"Almost all high school work should be done at school in school hours under guidance of teachers. Less assigned home work will mean less carrying of responsibility for school duties during the hours at home when often such responsibilities can not be met and under conditions which often foster ineffective habits of study. There will always remain plenty of good home work; good reading, some assignment, upon work in line with school work; but our pupils should no more carry home with them the larger burden of their school work than a good business man should take home with him his major business duties." —**Otis Caldwell**, "The Laboratory Method," *Popular Science Monthly* LXX (March 1913): 251

"[T]he most common amount of time devoted to study outside of school by pupils is five to eight hours the week—certainly not an excessive amount. As far as these figures go they support the contention of teachers that it is not the school work, as such, but the outside activities which cause the heavy drain on the pupil's resources." —**Irving King**, *The High-School Age*, 1914, 62–63

"Home study robs many a nervous child of the needed margin of sleep. It not only causes him to remain up later, but is likely to induce an excited condition of mind which is followed by superficial and disturbed sleep. Arithmetic lessons are especially unsuited for home assignments, but because of their quality of definiteness they are just the kind of homework with which children are most likely to be burdened." —**Lewis Terman**, *The Hygiene of the School Child*, 1914, 377

"Home study should be discerningly assigned. Most complaints from parents loosely object to the amount of home work required. Doubtless teachers have often made unreasonable demands; pupils below the fifth grade in most schools need little or no home study, with the gradual increase in the upper grades until an hour a day is not an unreasonable expectation for most eighth-grade pupils." —**S. E. Davis**, *The Work of the Teacher*, 1918, 235

HUMOR

"Children have what sometimes seems an unfortunate capacity to discover humor in situations. The teacher who has cultivated a corresponding sense of humor has established a strong bond with her class. She will do well to laugh with them and to help them find occasions for laughter. The teacher whose sense of humor rests on sound and broad foundations will never be laughed at unkindly by her pupils, but will increase her authority and dignity by recognizing and exhibiting this wholesome element of a well-rounded character." —**J. Frank Marsh**, *The Teacher Outside the School*, 1928, 95–96

IMAGINATION

"The part that imagination plays in education cannot be overestimated. By imagination the human being can go outside of the sense grasp, can picture that which lies beyond his own immediate environment. That world beyond, of everlasting change in nature and man, is a world that the imagination must reveal, else study is vain and profitless." —**Francis Parker**, *Talks on Pedagogics*, 1894, 160

INDEPENDENT THINKING

"[T]he fact that the school does not always develop self-reliance and the power of independent thinking is conceded by every one. How to carry on the routine work of the school without deadening the native intellectual interests and curbing overmuch the child's personality is a problem whose solution must be sought anew by every generation of teachers." —**Lewis Terman**, *The Hygiene of the School Child*, 1914, 400

"We need more and more to encourage the habit of independent work. We must hope as children pass through our school system that they will grow more and more independent in their statement of conclusions and of beliefs. We can never expect that boys and girls, or men and women, will reach conclusions on all of the questions which are of importance to them, but it ought to be possible, especially for those of more than usual capacity, to distinguish between the conclusions of a scientific investigation and the statements of a demagogue." —**George Strayer and Naomi Norsworthy**, *How to Teach*, 1922, 123

INDIVIDUAL DIFFERENCES

"No two classes are alike in abilities, and no two children of even the same parents are duplicates. How infinitely greater, then, must be the variations in personality of the forty or fifty individuals who have come to the present with all the wide range of conditioning factors that enter into life! The recognition of these individual differences must be fundamental in scientific education." —**Preston Search**, *The Ideal School, or Looking Forward*, 1902, 166

"By the time the pupils reach the end of the sixth year they are so divergent in their attainments and in their outlooks that the organization of the school must reflect this diversity. There must be different paths for the pupils to follow." —**Charles Judd**, *The Evolution of a Democratic School System*, 1918, 98

INDIVIDUALIZED INSTRUCTION

"There is a common and flippant charge made against the public graded school, that the individual is neglected, that all are recklessly run through the same mill, without regard to the personal peculiarities of the pupil or to the purpose of his life; that the alert and the sluggish mind receive the same stupefying potions—that to the future senator and the incipient slugger are administered the same dull and dismal doses of dreary didactics and deadening discourses." —**George Howland**, *Practical Hints for the Teachers of Public Schools*, 1899, 129

INITIATIVE

"Let the child use his own initiative; do not suppress independent efforts. Help him only when necessary. Do not let him blindly follow your suggestions." —**John J. B. Morgan**, *The Psychology of the Unadjusted School Child*, 1930, 72

LESSON PLANS

"The daily plan is now recognised as a necessity, and its absence as an indication of laxity, and generally of inefficiency. When the teacher will give helter-skelter instruction with intermissions of vituperation, the pupils will not be in the best condition to attend to the matter before them." —**Felix Arnold**, *Attention and Interest: A Study in Psychology and Education*, 1910, 239

"After long experience with lesson plans and the writing of plans by students, the writer has come to the conclusion that the less formal they can be made, the better for all concerned. . . . The lesson plan is a guess at what the teacher will have to do in the recitation. But it is only a guess, for the lesson may not work out the way the teacher planned it, unless the teacher holds the class to *his* plan and does not follow the *pupils'* leads." —**W. W. Charters**, *Methods of Teaching*, 1912, 415

"A lesson plan may be a help or a hindrance to a teacher, according to the way it is used. If the teacher, with plan-book before his eyes, follows it closely, disregarding the state of mind of his class, the questions asked, the unexpected knowledge or ignorance revealed, his plan has been an obstacle to good, live teaching. If on the contrary, the teacher fixes in his mind the ends he desires to reach, the place where the class is to begin, the large points of his outline, and the few questions which are to direct thought, he can, to a great extent, disregard the plan book and work face to face with the class, following the bendings of the pupils' thinking, and recognizing the value of the contributions made. He knows where he intends to go and the general direction in which he must travel." —**Lida Earhart**, *Types of Teaching*, 1915, 231

"The time spent in preparing detailed [lesson] plans for the principal's desk would usually be better spent in reading, working with pupils, getting acquainted with parents and children, resting, playing, or sleeping. If a teacher possesses so little interest and enthusiasm in her work that a submitted lesson plan is the only assurance a principal can have that any thought has been given to the work of the day, then the sooner such teacher is eliminated from the school the better it will be." —**Elwood P. Cubberley**, *The Principal and His School*, 1923, 392

POSTURE

"Training in posture or correct carriage of the body is coming to be recognized as an indispensible part of physical training. Posture determines the relative position of the different parts of the body. If it is habitually correct, all parts of the body are in the right position to perform their functions and to develop properly. Habitually wrong postures, in sitting, standing, or walking, hamper the normal action of the vital organs; they distort the bones and muscles and cause unsymmetrical growth. In some schools instruction and training in posture is made a distinct part of the daily work of the school, and pupils are rated in this subject as they are in conduct, school attendance, or in the various subjects of study, the rating being based on their habitual postures as they sit and stand in the school and on the observations of the physical director at times of special inspection." —**Calvin Kendall and George Mirick**, *How to Teach the Fundamental Subjects*, 1915, 311–12

"Teachers long ago learned to infer inattention from a physical slump, whatever may have caused the slump, and to regard the two commands 'Sit up, and pay attention' as practically inseparable. Educational science must consider that whatever makes sitting up easier makes the paying of attention more sure, and that habitual sitting up contributes to, if it is not actually essential to, habitual paying attention." —**Henry Eastman Bennett**, *School Posture and Seating*, 1928, 56

"No statistical social or psychological studies are required to demonstrate the moral effect of erect posture of the pupils upon a teacher or class at work. Nothing can be more stimulating or indicative of attention and esprit de corps than a class all sitting erect at work; nothing more surely indicates low-grade class work than a group slumped and sprawled and stooped in countless graceless positions. Few things are more irritating to a teacher than the sprawling boy." —**Henry Eastman Bennett**, *School Posture and Seating*, 1928, 57

PREACHING

"Preaching is wasted on children (it is sometimes wasted on their elders), and direct moral instruction is apt to tire; but instruction by example is very powerful, whether it be the living example of parents and teachers or the models derived from history and fiction." —**David Salmon**, *The Art of Teaching*, 1903, 38

PROJECT METHOD

"The criticism of schools and school curricula for their failure to give instruction which is practical, instruction along project lines, is due in large measure to the fact that we rarely eliminate from our textbooks but are constantly adding. It takes a long time to eliminate from the textbooks and courses of study operations and materials which have become obsolete. This situation is due in part to the lack of an opportunity to use the material of the curriculum in solving difficulties arising in their natural setting, in the pupil's home and school life. The project method eliminates obsolete material for it uses only such subject material is necessary for the solution of the project."
—**John Stevenson**, *The Project Method of Teaching*, 1922, 152–53

QUESTIONS

"Questions should be asked before pronouncing the pupil's name, a pause following each question. Promiscuous rather than fixed rotation in reaching pupils, stimulates attention. While an equal number of opportunities to contribute may not be given to all, since pupils differ widely in capacity to profit by participation, the bright should not monopolize, the dull should not be ignored. To encourage those whose intellectual morale is low, a judicious qualitative apportionment of questions is permissible so that an occasional moderate success is possible for all. A hurried manner or tone, and inflection indicating doubt or defiance of a pupil's ability exert a negative influence. Questions are to develop or test rather than to convict. The question directed toward an inattentive pupil off guard is an act of discipline, not of teaching."
—**S. E. Davis**, *The Technique of Teaching*, 1924, 27

READING ALOUD

[On reading aloud in the classroom] "How can a pupil simulate great enthusiasm for reading when the teacher and every other pupil in the class has the text open in front of them and is reading, if reading at all, to criticise his manner of reading. If any adult will put himself in such a position for an hour, and read to an audience which knows all about what he is reading, and is merely waiting for slips in expression to occur, I venture to say that he would be on the verge of nervous prostration." —**W. W. Charters**, *Methods of Teaching*, 1912, 71

SCHOOLWORK

"Children rarely work harder than the conditions require and if teachers prefer to do the work for them the pupils will not deprive them of the pleasure." —**Edgar James Swift**, *Learning and Doing*, 1914, 64

"[S]chool tasks, such as the writing of certain exercises, should never be employed as punishments for misconduct. Not only does this violate the principle that school work should not be regarded in the light of an affliction, but it is ordinarily illogical and has a damaging effect upon the penmanship and neatness of the pupil's work." —**Arthur C. Perry Jr.**, *Discipline as a School Problem*, 1915, 201

SEATING OF STUDENTS

"The pupils should be so seated that the work of separate classes shall interfere as little as possible. And the separate seats should be of such a character that no unnecessary fatigue, or strain, or curves of the spine may interfere with the activity of the child's attention. It is possible, of course, to have a good school with rude slab benches, but the less attention a child is forced to pay to splinters the more he may give to his letters." —**J. A. H. Keith**, *Elementary Education: Its Problems and Processes*, 1905, 102–3

SECURING ATTENTION

"Poor school practices that hinder attention are, for example, the requirement that a rigidly stiff bodily position be maintained, as though pupils, to borrow Compayré's phrase, were 'thinking statues'; also censuring or punishing a pupil in the presence of other pupils, which for the time being interrupts the whole school order; and the besetting sin of whispering, due to the fundamental instinct of communication when stimulated by idleness, for which there is no defence, and whose cure is either interesting occupation or voluntary restraint. These then, are the frequent hindrances to attention, the most of them capable of removal." —**Herman Harrell Horne**, *The Psychological Principles of Education*, 1909, 315–16

SELF-DEVELOPMENT

"[I]n education the process of self-development should be encouraged to the fullest extent. Children should be led to make their own investigations, and to draw their own inferences. They should be *told* as little as possible, and induced to *discover* as much as possible." —**Herbert Spencer**, *Education: Intellectual, Moral, and Physical*, 1860, 126

SELF-FULFILLING PROPHECY

"Good teaching inspires *confidence and courage* in the pupils. Nothing is to be gained by telling children that they are dull or backward. Probably four out of five laggards are failing more from *discouragement than lack of ability*. A thoughtless teacher was one day called by an uplifted hand to the desk of a glum-looking boy. Joe was having trouble again with his examples. 'O

Joe,' complained the teacher, 'you are so dull! I am afraid you will never learn arithmetic.' Now this was precisely what Joe himself feared, and the judgment of the teacher only drove the conviction more deeply into the soul of the disheartened boy. What Joe needed was sympathy and encouragement, and a teacher wise enough to find out the faulty place in his reasoning and to help remedy it. An army or a football team which enters a conflict expecting defeat is already half beaten, and a pupil who starts on a lesson sure he can not master it has already failed." —**George Betts and Otis Hall**, *Better Rural Schools*, 1914, 199

SKIPPING GRADES

"A common occurrence in school administration bears out this conclusion reached by experimental means. The child who skips a grade is ready at the end of three years to skip again, and the child who fails a grade is likely at the end of three years to fail again." —**George Strayer and Naomi Norsworthy**, *How to Teach*, 1922, 159

SOCIAL PROMOTION OF STUDENTS

"A pupil who has been two years in a grade should be peremptorily advanced without a question and any member of the eighth grade sixteen years of age passed to the high-school unexamined, that they may have the trial, at least, of a new teacher." —**George Howland**, *Practical Hints for the Teachers of Public Schools*, 1899, 165

"If the child is of over-age, he should never be degraded by being classified with children much smaller, but should be placed more nearly with those of the same age and general physical condition, where, by individual attention from the teacher and his absorption of higher influences around him, he will be lifted more rapidly to his proper place." —**Preston Search**, *An Ideal School or, Looking Forward*, 1902, 274

"The importance of the distinction between physiological age and chronological age is obvious. We have lately awakened to the fact that each year one child in six or seven fails of promotion; that the large majority drop out before reaching the high school; that the wholesale elimination involves boys to a greater extent than girls; that girls of a given age make better marks in their class work and in examinations than boys of the same age; that many weakly pupils break down in the effort to keep up with the class in which their chronological age places them—that education from bottom to top needs more than anything else to be individualized." — **Lewis Terman**, *The Hygiene of the School Child*, 1914, 67–68

"A study of the performances of the failures in Boise has convinced the entire force that the repeater is generally a quitter, and does about as poor work in his second attempt as in his first trial at the work of a given grade. The stamp of disapproval has been place upon him. He starts on his second attempt with a grievance against the teacher and the entire institution. The parents as well as the child feel injured, so that the teacher must combat both the antagonism of the home and the hostility of the pupil, who has been trained for failure and not for success, and who becomes either morbidly sensitive or brazenly indifferent. What the laggard would probably do as a repeater is therefore quite definitely known. If he were permitted to advance, he could hardly do worse and he might do better. It is less expensive and more human to promote him than it is to degrade him. This view of the situation is generally accepted in Boise. The standard for promoting the dull pupil is entirely individual. He is not compelled to do all the work of his present grade before he is permitted to pass to the next. He is even allowed to pass on without manifesting enough ability to justify the hope that he may be able to do the work of the advanced grade. The question is reduced to the one consideration: Would he do better if advanced than he would as a repeater?"
—*Special Report of the Boise Public Schools* (June 1915): 17–18, quoted by **Charles Judd** in *Introduction to the Scientific Study of Education*, 1918, 104–5

"So much has been written on the question of student progress or promotion that little needs to be said here. But any teacher who holds all degrees of intellects to the same pace, although they may be grouped together in the same grade, is an enemy to childhood. Moreover, the teacher who holds a pupil back in one or two subjects because such a student failed in the remaining subjects of the grade is also an enemy to childhood. Any act of the teacher or the administration that checks the spontaneity of the child or diverts it into improper channels is fundamentally harmful because it does violence to the laws of growth and development. The school cannot become what it should be until the promotion or progress of individuals is so arranged that the greatest energy of the pupils is released." —**Eugene C. Brooks**, *Education for Democracy*, 1919, 101

STUDENT DISCUSSIONS

"If we would teach our pupils to examine thoughtfully, to collate, compare, and judiciously decide, we must give them an opportunity to present their views, discussing with them their conclusions, meeting their criticisms and wrong deductions, not by our mere arbitrary dicta, but by more convincing arguments, wise enough, too, to confess our own errors when at fault, without attempts at unworthy subterfuge of feeling humiliation." —**George Howland**, *Practical Hints for Teachers of Public Schools*, 1899, 97

STUDENT PROMOTION

"Promotion, usually associated with marks, exercises its greatest force in the upper grades and is most effective near the end of the term. Unfortunately 'failure to pass' is by some teachers too constantly kept before pupils. With the child in whom it arouses greatest anxiety, failure to be promoted with his class represents nothing less than a breakup of his world. The teacher who is eternally threatening pupils with failure is using a cruel weapon so far as nervous or over-conscientious children are concerned, and a useless one for those less suggestible." —**S. E. Davis**, *The Work of the Teacher*, 1919, 119–20

SUCCESS

"Success is necessary to every human being. To live in an atmosphere of failure is tragedy to many. It is not a matter of intellectual attainment; not an intellectual matter at all but a moral matter. The boys and girls coming out of school clear-headed and with good bodies, who are resolute, who are determined to do and sure that they can do, will do more for themselves and for the world than those who come out with far greater intellectual attainments, but who lack confidence, who have not established the habit of success but within whom the school has established the habit of failure." —**Leonard Ayres**, *Laggards in Our Schools*, 1909, 220

"The school should be a place wherein intellectual and moral victories are won by children—won by fighting—but won. A school where the children are meeting more defeats than victories is no place to train American citizens to win in the struggle of life to which they are destined." —**Charles McKenny**, *The Personality of the Teacher*, 1910, 30–31

"Teach the child the habit of success. This comes by attacking the hard problems and persisting at a task, once it is begun, until success comes. By hard problems we do not mean impossible ones that preclude chance of success. Choose problems that hold out promise of achievement with a reasonable amount of effort, and then have the child put forth a little more energy than is necessary so that success will be assured. This can be accomplished in the physical sphere as well as in the mental; in sports as well as in study. The mental effect of any success is the same." —**John J. B. Morgan**, *The Psychology of the Unadjusted School Child*, 1930, 291

TAKING CHILDREN AS THEY ARE

"It is, of course, admitted that we must take children as they are. Complaint that they were not born right avails nothing. They are the raw material which must be worked up by the schools. Now there are at least two widely different ways of approaching our task. We may decide just what sort of men and women we would like to make out of them and then regulate their 'going and coming' by assignments of work, by rules and prohibitions with a view to developing our ideal type of adults. Or, again, instead of settling at the start the kind of men and women we will make our pupils into, we may supply incentives for the development of various sorts of ability. To illustrate our point somewhat roughly, if we were to rear a strange animal with whose habits of eating we were unacquainted, we should scatter various kinds of food before it to learn which it would select. This, indeed, is exactly our method when we read aloud to children from different books, taking care to stop each time at some interesting place to see which book is sufficiently absorbing for them to wish to continue it by themselves." —**Edgar James Swift**, *Learning and Doing*, 1914, 38

TAKING NOTES

"It will help pupils to keep to the point if they write in their notebooks the questions or topics they are to consider, and then, as important parts are brought out in the lesson, they should write these in order under the proper question or topic. Sometimes, when attention lags or wanders, the teacher needs to call it back by asking, 'What are we trying to find out just now?' or some similar question. The pupils will learn presently to criticize those who stray from the subject at hand." —**Lida Earhart**, *Types of Teaching*, 1915, 73

TAXONOMY OF QUESTIONS

"Questions are of five types: memory, analytic, developmental, comparison-contrast, and judgment." —**Herbert Foster**, *Principles of Teaching in Secondary Education*, 1921, 72

TEACHER TALK

"Teachers have a habit of monopolizing continued discourse. Many, if not most, instructors would be surprised if informed at the end of the day of the amount of time they have talked as compared with any pupil. Children's conversation is often confined to answering questions in brief phases, or in single disconnected sentences. Expatiation and explanation are reserved for the teacher, who often admits any hint at an answer on the part of the pupil, and then amplifies what he supposes the child must have meant. The habits of sporadic and fragmentary discourse thus promoted have inevitably a disintegrating intellectual influence." —**John Dewey**, *How We Think*, 1910, 185–86

TEACHING

"[A]lways remember that to educate rightly is not a simple and easy thing, but a complex and extremely difficult thing: the hardest task which devolves upon adult life." —**Herbert Spencer**, *Education: Intellectual, Moral, and Physical*, 1860, 231

"The teacher should be able to tell why he teaches arithmetic or history, and why he teaches them in a certain way, as the physician should be able to tell why he prescribes dieting and exercise for certain ailments, and this drug for other diseases. Just as the physician should know the specific effect of any medicine upon the organs of the body, so the teacher should know the effect of a given school exercise or branch of study on the different faculties of the mind." —**Ruric Roark**, *Psychology in Education*, 1895, 7

"It cannot be too often repeated that teaching bears no likeness to the mechanic arts where rigid rules and exact measurements are required. It is even doubtful whether procedure by fixed rule is ever permissible in real teaching." —**W. H. Payne**, *The Education of Teachers*, 1901, 28

"If the teacher knows his subjects thoroughly, is earnest and impressive; if he understands his pupils and knows how to select and present suitable material; if he is so fully master of method as not to be fettered by it, but to be set free by making it his instrument and his aid; if he possesses the peculiar sympathy that attracts childhood and has the ability to enter into the thoughts and life of the child,–then his method is likely to be good and his instruction successful." —**Levi Seeley**, *Elementary Pedagogy*, 1906, 109–10

"The term 'teaching' has come to be used so loosely as to include almost everything a teacher does in the classroom. In the following discussions it is used to mean the stimulation of genuine constructive thinking directed toward a definite and desired end. This is accomplished in the main by thought-provoking questions. It is rarely accomplished by telling, by memorizing texts, or by lecturing, followed by testing. This meaning is in accord with modern educational theory but is rarely found in practice. Memory and test questions dominate the whole range of classroom work. It is not uncommon, indeed, for teachers of method, even of special method, to lecture and test, thus violating the most fundamental principle involved." —**John William Hall and Alice Cynthia King Hall**, *The Question as a Factor in Teaching*, 1916, 1

"So long has our profession taught that we think the only way to educate is *to teach*. We have not sufficiently known that *to live* will also educate. We have been busy providing the conditions for teaching. Only recently are we coming to know how to provide the conditions for living. Both have a place; and the main thing is living." —**Franklin Bobbitt**, *The Curriculum*, 1918, 243

"Nowhere is there as great need of the accelerator as in education. The teacher was educated yesterday, the children must be educated for to-morrow. Can one imagine the ability of one who was educated in 1910 teaching children in 1920 to be equipped for action in 1930?" —**A. E. Winship**, *Danger Signals for Teachers*, 1919, 29

TEACHING AND LEARNING

"Teaching and learning are correlative or corresponding processes, as much so as selling and buying. One might as well say he has sold when no one has bought, as to say that he has taught when no one has learned. And in the educational transaction, the initiative lies with the learner even more than in commerce it lies with the buyer." —**John Dewey**, *How We Think*, 1910, 29

TEACHING AS LEADERSHIP

"Fundamentally, teaching is leadership. It is essentially the art of stimulating and guiding the activity of another person's mind. You cannot inject an idea into a pupil's mental circulation as the doctor hypodermically injects drugs into the blood. The only thing that you can do is to lead him to center his attention on the idea which you wish him to get, by arousing his interest in it. There your power stops, and the pupil's mind must do the rest. The teacher is then an energizer and a guide. He arouses and directs the mental activities of his pupils." —**Charles McKenny**, *The Personality of the Teacher*, 1910, 49

"The union of the terms 'good teaching' and 'effective learning' gives a clue to what teaching is at basis. To stimulate, encourage, and direct learning is the soul and substance of the art of teaching. It is the pupil himself who must learn. Without activity on the student's part,–without some dynamic expression of a 'will to learn,'—the efforts of the best teachers will be futile." —**William Chandler Bagley and John Keith**, *An Introduction to Teaching*, 1929, 27

TEXTBOOKS

"[C]onsider the text-book a guide to be understood, not an authority to be memorized. This for teacher and pupil alike. For the teacher to dare to disagree, and to know enough to do so successfully, will mark an era in that class-room. Be continually making contributions to the text; your pupils will thrive in such a bracing atmosphere. The real teacher is not the teacher of a book, but the teacher of the truth, using books only to supplement his teaching." —**Herman Harrell Horne**, *The Psychological Principles of Education*, 1909, 173–74

"The slavish use of textbooks is largely to blame for the inefficiency of teachers in giving assignments and hearing recitations, as well as the overcrowded condition of our schools, which forces many good teachers to do their work in a mechanical way. They hear recitations. Our texts are usually good, but in the hands of teachers who shift to them the whole responsibility of instruction, they are a source of weakness, not of strength. Good texts can never take the place of good teachers. As professional training increases, the evil of textbook dependence will be reduced. Probably most teachers have remarked that if nine things be studied from a book and a tenth told by the teacher, the tenth fact is the one that is remembered on examination day—or any other day." —**Frances Morehouse**, *The Discipline of the School*, 1914, 228

"It is generally recognized that in most schools textbooks determine the methods of teaching probably more than any other factor." —**Thomas Briggs**, *The Junior High School*, 1920, 208

TIME ON TASK

"Scientific measurement of the results achieved in a large number of class groups spending varying amounts of time in a given subject may give teachers this knowledge. In 1902 Dr. J. M. Rice, in the measurement of the ability of 6000 children in seven different school systems, found no direct relationship between the time devoted in a school to arithmetic and the results achieved by the children." —**George Strayer and N. L. Engelhardt**, *The Classroom Teacher at Work in American Schools*, 1920, 217

TONE

"The most vital and determining quality of a school is its tone or atmosphere—the spirit which pervades it. You may strike the same note on a tin pan that a violinist sounds on his instrument, but what a difference in quality! Yet the difference is no greater than may be noticed between two schoolrooms presided over by teachers of different temperament but equally well disposed." —**Charles McKenny**, *The Personality of the Teacher*, 1910, 17–18

TYPES OF LEARNERS

"There is also great difference between the general mental make-up of children—a difference in type. There is the child who excels in dealing with abstract ideas. He usually has power also in dealing with the concrete, but his chief interest is in the abstract. He is the one who does splendid work in mathematics, formal grammar, the abstract phases of the sciences. Then there is the child who is a thinker too, but his best work is done when he is dealing with a concrete situation. Unusual or involved applications of principles disturb him. So long as his work is couched in terms of the concrete, he can succeed, but if that is replaced by the x, y, z elements, he is prone to fail." —**George Strayer and Naomi Norsworthy**, *How to Teach*, 1922, 163

WAIT TIME

"Many a child is rebuked for 'slowness,' for not 'answering promptly,' when his forces are taking time to gather themselves together to deal effectively with the problem at hand. In such cases, failure to afford time and leisure conduce to habits of speedy, but snapshot and superficial, judgment. The depth to which a sense of the problem, of the difficulty, sinks, determines the quality of the thinking that follows; and any habit of teaching which encourages the pupil for the sake of a successful recitation or of a display of memorized information to glide over the thin ice of genuine problems reverses the true method of mind training." —**John Dewey**, *How We Think*, 1910, 38

WITH-IT-NESS

"The teacher's eye, indeed, is the controlling force in the class-room, as it is in the presence of any audience. The difference between an old hand and a beginner in teaching is shown most markedly in the power the former has of *seeing* everything that goes on in the room. The beginner has not learnt to adjust his powers: all his attention is taken up with his own utterance, or with the answer by one pupil. The experienced teacher hears this answer, but at the same time he sees an inattentive rascal in the far corner, he notes how the time is passing, and has a spare thought for the next item in his Presentation. Experience in an art alone enables the artist to do half-a-dozen things at once. As a hint by way of learning these habits, young teachers may be advised never to trouble to look at the pupil who is giving a reply, but at *others* in the class. Your ears are sufficient to attend to *him* with; let your eyes help the rest of the class to keep in touch." —**J. J. Findlay**, *Principles of Class Teaching*, 1911, 393

Chapter Five

Curriculum

As schools became larger and more comprehensive the curriculum began to grow. There was concern about how rapidly the public school curriculum was expanding. The concern was that the schools were trying to do too much. As more subjects were added to the curriculum, it was felt there was little time for in- depth study for any subject—that education was becoming superficial.

Many school districts developed standard courses of study. Critics were concerned that the standard course of study allowed little instructional freedom for teachers; schools were becoming too formalized and inflexible which did not support individualized student growth. In addition, with the standardized course of study, the curriculum was always slow to change.

CREDIT FOR HOME ACTIVITIES

"[T]he extension of school supervision is illustrated by the fact that in a township high school the girls who are taking cooking are required to do each day a certain amount of laboratory work in the kitchen at home. This is reported by the parents, and the cooking teacher visits the homes from time to time to inspect the work. Again, in many agricultural schools home gardening is required as a part of the course. Sometimes a school officer is employed to keep up the supervision of this home work during the vacation period. Another series of examples under this heading is to be found in those systems where miscellaneous home activities are credited by the school on the report of parents." —**Charles Judd**, *Introduction to the Scientific Study of Education*, 1918, 142

CURRICULUM

"The curriculum may, therefore, be defined in two ways: (1) it is the entire range of experiences, both undirected and directed, concerned in unfolding the abilities of the individual; or (2) it is the series of consciously directed training experiences that the schools use for completing and perfecting the unfoldment. Our profession uses the term usually in the latter sense. But as education is coming more and more to be seen as a thing of experiences, and as the work-and play-experiences of the general community life are being more and more utilized, the line of demarcation between directed and undirected training experience is rapidly disappearing. Education must be concerned with both, even though it does not direct both." —**Franklin Bobbitt**, *The Curriculum*, 1918, 43

CURRICULUM CHANGE

"The ultimate source of authority in determining the content of the curriculum must lie in the needs and demands of society. What the social process requires the curriculum must contain. When society outlives old ideals and enters upon new lines of experience, the curriculum must change in conformity with the new conditions. In all progressive societies, therefore, the curriculum will be in a constant state of reconstruction. If the curriculum proves unable to make this readjustment in accordance with changing social demands, and continues in traditional but outgrown lines, it obstructs instead of furthering social progress." —**George Herbert Betts**, *Social Principles of Education*, 1912, 256

"The curriculum of a school is a living thing. It is constantly undergoing readjustments. Its content is drawn from the social life to which it introduces pupils, and its arrangement depends on the ability of pupils of different ages and different capacities to grasp this constantly readjusted content. There are some teachers who prefer to have the course of study handed down to them by some superior authority." —**Charles Judd**, *Introduction to the Scientific Study of Education*, 1918, 197.

"The characteristic fact about the present generation of progressive educators is that they are undertaking certain studies which are designed to hasten the processes of selection. The curriculum is to be modified and improved, with every new accession of knowledge and with every new evolution in social life. How the improvement can be brought about most expeditiously and most productively is a problem which is engaging much of the attention and energy of school officers." —**Charles Judd**, *Introduction to the Scientific Study of Education*, 1918, 200

"Indeed, it may be said that a change in the curriculum runs on the average ten years behind the advocating of a change in the aim of education. And for the curriculum change to become large enough to be noticed, a much longer period of incubation is necessary." —**W. W. Charters**, *Curriculum Construction*, 1923, 5

CURRICULUM DEVELOPMENT

"Teachers of unusual ability, who have a genuine interest in the problems of the curriculum, should, from time to time, be excused from their regular classroom work in order to spend their time in coöperation with supervisors in the development of courses of study." —**George Strayer and N. L. Engelhardt**, *The Classroom Teacher at Work in American Schools*, 1920, 56

CURRICULUM EXPANSION

"In our common schools we try to do too much, and we do not do well what we seek to do. We lose from view the aim that we ought to have, namely, the action of the children's minds. We hurry our boys and girls from one study to another, from one 'grade' to the next, and we are not sufficiently careful as to whither, when they have 'gone through' these, they can make any real use of the knowledge they been pursuing." —**Edward Cary**, "An Evil of the Schools," *The Forum* VI (June 1887): 419–20

"Additions [to the curriculum] have been made, from time to time…until the curriculum of many schools is over-crowded with a great number of unrelated subjects, arranged with little or no regard to logical or psychological order. No effort has been made, in most cases, to correlate or coordinate the difference branches of study." [Putnam goes on to make the case for an integrated curriculum]. —**Daniel Putnam**, *Manual of Pedagogics*, 1899, 269

"In the struggle to 'teach' everything that is now demanded, the school is forced to give almost every subject a superficial treatment. This is wrong both from the standpoint of school economy and from the standpoint of mental development." —**William Chandler Bagley**, *Classroom Management*, 1911, 69

"The curriculum has in recent years grown not only vastly richer and more interesting, but much fuller, as well. The broadening of education and the demand for studies of a more practical type have thus placed an increasing burden on both pupil and teacher. So much material has been added that the elementary course of study now includes a greater variety and amount of subject-matter than was required for admission to college several generations ago. And the high-school graduate of to-day has certainly been forced to cover more ground than was demanded to graduate from Harvard at the time when Longfellow was a member of the faculty." —**George Betts and Otis Hall**, *Better Rural Schools*, 1914, 77

"Social changes which have left many units of subject matter without function have also developed much new and exceedingly valuable material which is gradually being incorporated into the curriculum.History, physiology, drawing, music, manual training, and elementary science under various names have been added to the elementary school curriculum; music appreciation, sex-instruction, physical education, agriculture and other forms of prevocational education, as well as moral training and vocational guidance, are now presenting their claims. Elimination has not proceeded as rapidly as addition and the overcrowded curriculum is the result; pupils are accused of attempting too many things and of doing nothing well." —**S. E. Davis**, *The Work of the Teacher*, 1918, 44

"At times ingenious groups of teachers and scholars organized groups of subject-matter far beyond the needs of their time. Interested in the pursuit of knowledge for its own sake, they formulated rules, laws, and principles that they thought were true. The subject-matter then was organized around these, and when the task was finished, the average man hardly recognized the results as related to his needs. Some types of minds enjoyed such thinking, and it sometimes happened that subjects thus organized were preserved and handed down in the schools for generations....Although they started as a phase of man's social needs, they became so modified later that they were of little value in providing for these needs." —**Charles Holley**, *The Teacher's Technique*, 1924, 41–42

CURRICULUM RESPONSE

"Briefly stated, the curriculum has been slow to respond to the changing statements of the aim of education because (1) those who have formulated the aims of education have not taken into account the activities which individuals carry on. Rather have they laid stress merely upon ideals from which a curriculum can be derived. As the result of this failure, (2) the curriculum has been under the domination of the idea that the youth should be given a birds-eye view of the knowledge of the world rather than a compendium of useful information. Furthermore, (3) when the material in this curriculum has been criticised as lacking practicalness, the school administrators, with whom the defence of the curriculum rests, have until quite recently justified it by an appeal to the doctrines of formal discipline and the transfer of training." —**W. W. Charters**, *Curriculum Construction*, 1923, 4

EXPERIENTIAL EDUCATION

"There has been and still persists the conception that education is a classroom affair; that only what can be taken care of at the school-building is to be done; that educational specialists are not to lead or direct or be otherwise concerned with experiences which must be had in other places within the community. The present topic more than any other discussed in this volume reveals the limitations of such primitive educational thought and practice."
—**Franklin Bobbitt**, *The Curriculum*, 1918, 180

"Experiential education aims at the greatest possible educational efficiency, substantiality, and practicality of result. It employs interest for the sake of vividness and massiveness of experience; not for the sake of pleasantness. It *uses* pleasantness as a means; not as an end." —**Franklin Bobbitt**, *The Curriculum*, 1918, 236

INFLUENCE OF COLLEGES

"The time is rapidly passing when the colleges can dictate what shall be the education in the secondary schools." —**Preston Search**, *The Ideal School or, Looking Forward*, 1902, 154

MORAL EDUCATION

"Moral teaching in the schools is impossibility; for it is generally agreed that religion, in the ordinary sense of the word, shall not be taught in schools supported by the state." —**Daniel Putnam**, *A Manual of Pedagogics*, 1899, 28

MORE VS. BETTER SCHOOLING

"The school year has already doubled or trebled in length, and more and better books and courses of study have been added. The course has certainly been greatly, perhaps too much, enriched. But all this increase of book-work and of learning does not meet the difficulty which we are considering; it probably increases it. Especially in the lower grades the child is kept over his books longer than he should be. We overexercise his brain, while we cramp his muscles. The result is that he learns to dislike books, and to form the worst possible habits of study. These habits often become so fixed as to be practically unchangeable. In the schools of many of our towns and cities the child is engaged in mental work nearly throughout the session; at least, he is supposed to be busied. Yet often he acquires no more learning than the child who goes to school only one half of the day. He probably learns much less than the average child would under the system of the industrial schools where outdoor work and manual training occupy a large part of the time." — **John Mason Tyler**, *Growth and Education*, 1907, 249

RELEVANCE

"Manual training schools would do for the boy in town what the farm did for his father, and more,–they would engage him in an activity which he would like, and in the prosecution of which he would have to coordinate his powers in the attainment of definite ends. He would be compelled to save his energies for this purpose, and not squander them in riotous living. Greek and algebra and parsing alone will never keep the village boy from drink and things worse; such a curriculum is liable to drive him out of school on to the street. Everything in the schools ought to have an obvious life relation for the boy who has passed his twelfth birthday. He must feel that in mastering any study he is gaining real power, which he will find of service in the world outside." —**M. V. O'Shea**, *Social Development and Education*, 1909, 391

"A boy just graduated from high school came to his principal and said: 'I have finished the work of the school. What am I to do now?' The principal said with a grandiloquent flourish: 'We have led you out upon the broad sea of opportunity, and you can now steer your ship in any direction you choose. You are prepared to do anything.' The youth replied with a touch of bitterness, 'It seems to me you have led me out into a bank of fog.' We are . . . beginning to see that the youth was right." —**Irving King**, *Social Aspects of Education*, 1913, 177

SOCIALIZING THE CURRICULUM

"The expressions, 'Socializing the curriculum,' 'Socializing the school procedure,' are current to-day. The pupils are not merely to have the mental processes, such as reasoning, memory, and attention, trained, but are to live as members of a society, and are, in learning, to socialize the subject-matter; that is, to give it a social context, to see how man has affected it, how it affects man, and to learn the social purposes it serves. This changed view of the school is far-reaching in its effects." —**Lida Earhart**, *Types of Teaching*, 1915, 131

THE STANDARD COURSE OF STUDY

"The greatest trouble with our educational system to-day is that it is laid out too much on the plan of a trunk line railroad without side switches or way stations, but with splendid terminal facilities, so that we send the educational trains thundering over the country, quite oblivious of the population except to take on passengers, and these we take on much as the fast train takes mail bags from the hook. We do our utmost to keep them aboard, to the end, and we work so exclusively for this purpose that those who leave us are fitted for no special calling, and drop out for no special purpose, but roll off like chunks of coal by the wayside—largely a matter of luck as to what becomes of them. I would reconstruct the policy of the system by making all trains local, both to take on and *leave off passengers;* and I would pay much attention to the sidings, and the depots, and their surroundings at the way stations, to the end that those who do not complete the journey may find congenial surroundings and useful employment in some calling along the line." —**E. Davenport**, *Education for Efficiency*, 1914, 27–28

"It is often claimed by the critics of the public schools that teachers are not allowed any freedom in the use of the course of study; that all pupils in the same grade in all of the schools, regardless of conditions, are compelled to be at the same place in the study of the same subject on the same day; that all classes of the same grade must do exactly the same amount of work in a specified time, whatever their abilities may be; that teachers of ten-talent, five talent, and one-talent schools must all render the same amount of their stewardship; and that as a result not only individual pupils, but entire classes of pupils, are either stretched or contracted to meet the absolutely unchangeable demands of an absolutely fixed course of study." —**Oscar Corson**, *Our Public Schools: Their Teachers, Pupils, and Patrons*, 1918, 147–48

"Even in school systems where the course of study is rigidly outlined, and even based on definite page assignments in definite textbooks, the principal will still find it possible to suggest some points for omission or emphasis, and to help teachers, especially new ones, to plan out the term's work for their classes. The problem then is not only to try to modify, where possible, with a view to providing as intelligent instruction for the pupils as can be done, but also to inject as much stimulus to thinking as is possible for the teachers, despite the rigidity of the instruction. There is always the greatest danger, under such a system, of the teachers becoming mechanical workers and the covering of the course of study becoming the end and aim of the work." — **Elwood P. Cubberley**, *The Principal and His School*, 1923, 388–89

Chapter Six

Education

Writers spent a great deal of time thinking about what it meant to be educated. For some, education was the vehicle that allowed children to rise to a higher moral order. Education taught children how to develop character and good work habits so they could become productive adults. For most writers education was preparation for the future; the notable exception was John Dewey who proposed that education was not a preparation for life, education was life. Children should not be thought of as future adults, they were engaged in life activities in the present, during childhood. Dewey also made a distinction between education and schooling.

Many topics were discussed as educational issues. Some of these topics included the feminization of education, what to do about immigrant children, the federal role in education, multicultural classrooms, the role of religion, and a number of other issues. There was a new sense of pride in American education and what it was trying to accomplish.

Although when Lewis Terman, who had been a health educator before his involvement with I.Q. testing and gifted education, proposed that schools feed hungry children he was met with the criticism that introducing food programs in schools was a form of socialism.

DEMOCRACY IN EDUCATION

"The educational meaning of democracy is that every child shall have both incentive and opportunity to carry his educational development as far as his ability and circumstances will warrant, and in such direction as his taste, capacity, and situation in life may make desirable. For in education what is best for the individual is also best for society." —**Charles DeGarmo**, *Principles of Secondary Education*, 1909, 1

EDUCATION IS . . .

"Education may be defined as the development of the attitude of the being towards truth." —**Francis Parker**, *Talks on Pedagogics*, 1894, 139

"I believe that education . . . is a process of living and not a preparation for future living." —**John Dewey**, "My Pedagogic Creed," *The Elementary School Journal* LIV (January 1897), 77

"Education is the process of bringing a human being into likeness with the highest type of his kind." —**W. H. Payne**, *The Education of Teachers*, 1901, 243

"If education cannot be identified with mere instruction, what is it? What does the term mean? I answer, it must mean a gradual adjustment to the spiritual possessions of the race. Those possessions may be variously classified, but they certainly are at least five-fold. The child is entitled to his scientific inheritance, to his literary inheritance, to his æsthetic inheritance, to his institutional inheritance, and to his religious inheritance. Without them he cannot become a truly educated or a cultivated man." —**Nicholas Murray Butler**, *The Meaning of Education*, 1903, 17

"Education is the most universal concern of mankind because (1) it touches and relates to every phase of human activity, and (2) it is a process which continues in time from the cradle to the grave." —**John Alexander Hull Keith**, *Elementary Education: Its Problems and Processes*, 1905, 11

"Education is not a word confined rigidly to specified occupations of man, but refers vaguely to more or less of human activity in the production and prevention of changes in the production and prevention of changes in other human beings. In the broadest sense, man is an educator in every act that changes any other man." —**E. L. Thorndike**, *Education: A First Book*, 1912, 2

"Education is more than schooling. It calls for the latent powers of childhood, and the primitive instincts are among the resources at the disposal of the teacher. By utilizing them they become allies for promoting growth, instead of obstacles to be overcome, and the enthusiasm created by their recognition as springs of action in the young gives zest to work that makes it pleasant, though not easy." —**Edgar James Swift**, *Learning and Doing*, 1914, 34–35

"[Education] is that reconstruction or reorganization of experience which adds to the meaning of experience, and which increases ability to direct future experience." —**John Dewey**, *Democracy and Education*, 1916, 89–90

"When all the definitions of education and its ultimate aim which have been proposed by great educators and philosophers have been examined, it will be found they all agree that the supreme purpose of education is character-building, and the ultimate result character. If teachers would recognize this fact more fully than they generally do, they would understand that education must show its result in the character of the individual rather than in the amount of objective knowledge he acquires, and they would strive more for the subjective result in the character of the individual. This does not suggest that the objective matter is not to be presented, nor that subjective and objective teaching are widely separated and inharmonious processes. On the contrary, the objective elements are necessary and must be correlated with the subjective, for a person can arrive at a knowledge of self only through a knowledge of things external to himself." —**O. I. Woodley and M. Virginia Woodley**, *The Profession of Teaching*, 1917, 59

"The real purpose in education, aside from the learning of a few facts and the mastery of certain abilities that are found to be of use in later life, is to train young people how to analyze a problem and find out things for themselves; to form in them good working habits; to show them how to concentrate attention and to study effectively and independently; to teach them how to gather facts and marshal them to form a conclusion; and to awaken in them motives for work beyond what the school requires." —**Elwood P. Cubberley**, *The Principal and His School*, 1923, 401

"Education is primarily for adult life, not for child life. Its fundamental responsibility is to prepare for the fifty years of adulthood, not for the twenty years of childhood and youth." —**Franklin Bobbitt**, *How to Make a Curriculum*, 1924, 8

"[E]ducation . . . is to fit an individual to become successful in his personal relations with his fellows. Any educational system which does this is doing a real service for its students; any system which makes its students less able to secure the love and friendship of other human beings is a failure. A well-balanced curriculum is one which gives a man the maximum advantage in the race for social recognition, and the narrow or unbalanced curriculum is the one which leaves him with a loophole in his character, so furnishing a handicap against which he must constantly battle. The success of an educational institution should be measured not by the facility with which the seniors can make orations or solve mathematical problems, but by the social adjustability of its alumni." —**John J. B. Morgan**, *The Psychology of the Unadjusted School Child*, 1930, 7

EDUCATION VS. SCHOOLING

"What is learned in school is at the best only a small part of education, a relatively superficial part; and yet what is learned in school makes artificial distinctions in society and marks persons off from one another. Consequently we exaggerate school learning compared with what is gained in the ordinary course of living." —**John and Evelyn Dewey**, *Schools of To-morrow*, 1915, 2

"Facts which are not led up to out of something which has previously occupied a significant place for its own sake in the child's life, are apt to be barren and dead. They are hieroglyphics which the pupil is required to study and learn while he is school. It is only after the child has learned the same fact out of school, in the activities of real life, that it begins to mean anything to him." —**John and Evelyn Dewey**, *Schools of To-morrow*, 1915, 73

EDUCATIONAL DECISION MAKING

"The fact is that, despite the hundreds of thousands of trained workers in education and the millions of treasure freely spent each year, we still base our actions in education largely on opinion, guess work and eloquence." —**Leonard Ayres**, *Laggards in Our Schools*, 1909, 219

EDUCATIONAL PANACEAS

"We are prone to think that in some one new method of teaching, or method of discipline, or method of classification and promotion, we have found a panacea for all the educational ills we have known." —**Olive Jones**, *Teaching Children to Study*, 1909, 12

FAITH IN EDUCATION

"Like all simple and unsophisticated peoples we Americans have a sublime faith in education. Faced with any difficult problem of life we set our minds at rest sooner or later by the appeal to the school. We are convinced that education is the one unfailing remedy for every ill to which man is subject, whether it be vice, crime, war, poverty, riches, injustice, racketeering, political corruption, race hatred, class conflict, or just plain original sin. We even speak glibly and often about the general reconstruction of society through the school. We cling to this faith in spite of the fact that the very period in which our troubles have multiplied so rapidly has witnessed an unprecedented expansion of organized education. This would seem to suggest that our schools, instead of directing the course of change, are themselves driven by the very forces that are transforming the rest of the social order." —**George Counts**, *Dare the School Build a New Social Order?* 1932, 3

FEDERAL ROLE IN EDUCATION

"A bill now before Congress provides for the reestablishment of a Department of Education and a Secretary of Education in the President's Cabinet. It further provides that the United States Government shall subsidize certain types of education that the states have not as yet adequately provided for. These are the removal of illiteracy, the Americanization of the foreigner, physical education, and the preparation of an adequate number of teachers. The bill also provides an appropriation to help equalize the cost of education among several states. A determined fight for this bill is being waged by a large group of teachers and administrators." —**George Frasier and Winfred Armentrout**, *An Introduction to Education*, 1924, 215

FEMINIZATION OF EDUCATION

"The prophecies of evil effects from the feminization of the teaching staff of elementary and secondary schools that have been made have not been verified by facts. . . . The only clear probability of harm done by the present use of educational funds to hire women rather than men lies in the prevention of gifted and devoted women from having and rearing children of their own flesh and blood. Effectiveness from the narrow point of view of schoolroom education may be consistent with injury, small or great, to the life of the country as a whole. It is certainly risky to have over half of the graduates of women's colleges remain childless by profession, even if they spend their time working for the children of others. It is likely that the world loses more by the absence from motherhood of women teachers who might otherwise marry than by the absence from the teaching profession of the men who would have their places." —**E. L. Thorndike**, *Education: A First Book*, 1912, 158–59

HISTORY OF EDUCATION

"The history of education presents many of the great problems that have interested thoughtful men, shows how some of these have been solved, points the way to the solution of others. It studies educational systems, selecting the good, and rejecting the bad, and introducing the student directly to the pedagogical questions that have influenced the world. For these reasons, the study of education should begin with its history." —**Levi Seeley**, *History of Education*, 1899, 15

"When so much is said and written about 'fads and frills' and a return to the 'fundamentals' of the 'good old days,' school people must know educational history in order to evaluate accurately the new and the old. For adequate analysis the problems of class size, individualized instruction, and progressive education require the contribution of the educational historian. When legislatures are passing drastic school laws, which inevitably must be changed when the members are saner, wiser, and less panicky, the efforts of the relatively small group of research workers in the field of school legislation should be extended more than ever. Suggestions or commands for changes in curriculum, organization, or method, dictated by the voice of legislative or executive authority, born of necessity or panic, must be tested experimentally in actual school situations for any worth-while evaluation." —**Carter V. Good, A. S. Barr, and Douglas Scates**, *The Methodology of Educational Research*, 1935, 33–34

IMMIGRATION EDUCATION

"The American school should become as much the school for the foreign parent as for the child of foreign parentage." —**George Strayer and N. L. Engelhardt**, *The Classroom Teacher at Work in American Schools*, 1920, 372

"Immigration is our oldest social problem, and is basic, for many of our fundamental difficulties issue from this source. The problem of Americanization, the melting pot theories are centered here. The schools have a major part to play in this process of making Americans out of those who come to us with social backgrounds different from our native *mores*. —**A. O. Bowden**, "Our 396 Major Social Problems and Issues and the Schools," *Journal of Educational Sociology* 2 (March 1929): 400–1

MULTICULTURAL EDUCATION

"[C]ountries like the United States are composed of a combination of different groups with different customs. It is this situation which has, perhaps more than any other one cause, forced the demand for an educational institution which shall provide something like a homogeneous and balanced environment for the young. Only in this way can the centrifugal forces set up by juxtaposition of different groups within one and the same political unit be counteracted. The intermingling in the school of youth of different races, differing religions, and unlike customs creates for all a new and broader environment. Common subject matter accustoms all to a unity of outlook upon a broader horizon than is visible to the members of any group while it is isolated. The assimilative force of the American public school is eloquent testimony to the efficacy of the common and balanced appeal." —**John Dewey**, *Democracy and Education*, 1916, 25–26

THE NATIONAL EDUCATIONAL ASSOCIATION

"For thirty years the National Educational Association has been known as a large body of teachers that assembled annually to listen to addresses and discussions of more or less practical value. It has come to command an attendance of as many as sixteen thousand teachers, of all classes and from every section of the country. Its power and authority have increased with its size and its representative character." —**Nicholas Murray Butler**, *The Meaning of Education*, 1903, 190

THE NEW EDUCATION

"It may therefore be seen that the new education recognizes that there are elements aside from measurable results that require consideration in educating the child. The first and foremost among these elements is the child himself. The old system of education thinks only of the results, and with its eye upon the results, forgets the child." —**Joseph Mayer Rice**, *The Public School System of the United States*, 1893, 22

PRIDE IN AMERICAN EDUCATION

"Once having conceived of education as the birthright of every American boy and girl, we have in time worked out this conception in a series of free, non-sectarian, tax supported schools that, despite all their deficiencies, stand forth as examples of the creative achievement of the American people in other than material things. We still have much to do before our schools can be considered thoroughly satisfactory, and many poor schools and poorly prepared teachers are still found among us; nevertheless there are in the United States some of the best schools and some of the best teachers to be found anywhere in the world. Our schools may lack the evenness that characterizes the older European schools, and our teachers the uniform training that distinguishes the teachers of the more advanced European nations, yet our better schools and our better teachers are the envy of visitors from abroad. Discerning individuals and commissions coming to the United States to try to find the secret of our large creative power have attributed much of our national progress and development to the work of our teachers." —**Elwood P. Cubberley**, *A Distinctive American Achievement*, 1926, 2

PURPOSE OF EDUCATION

"The scheme of education that has grown up in America suggests that school training is primarily for those who are planning to enter the 'learned professions.' The elementary school prepares for high school, and the high school prepares for college. Those who have no interest in this line of progress show signs of practical intelligence when they drop out of school and go to work as soon as the law will allow them to do so." —**Marion Trabue**, *Measuring Results in Education*, 1924, 435

REGIMENTATION OF SCHOOLING

"From the kindergarten up through the high school, one is impressed by the breathlessness of this process we call education. With clocklike precision the kindergarten children draw with crayons for fifteen minutes, build with blocks for another fifteen minutes, sing their songs, drink their milk, and rest; all to the accurate timing of a watch. With the same monotonous haste, a sixth grade class of forty boys and girls races through a meaningless program of, successively, drill spelling an English lesson (sentence analysis on a particular day of 'Her the gods loved and blest, with the flower of youth and beauty'), a history lesson of rote memory sentences about the Gallic Wars, and then are trotted off to calisthenics. The pupils are hurried because the teacher constantly prompts them to be quicker in their responses; the teacher prompts because she is told to finish a given amount of text in a limited amount of time; and she is so instructed because it is necessary that all classes keep abreast of each other or confusion in the administration of so large a group ensues. And so the mechanizing chain goes on. Institutionalism, even the supposed institutionalism of individuation, wants conformity! And the end result is wholesale methods, quantity production, and an 'educated' product as different from what it could have been as modern stamped-out furniture is different from the lovingly wrought masterpieces of the medieval craftsman-artist." —**James Woodard**, "Education as a Social Problem," *Journal of Educational Sociology* 6 (January 1933): 300–1

RELIGION IN EDUCATION

"The attempt to divorce God from education is our American idea. The result is not much to boast of. Irreverence, profanity, dishonesty, and the deep ingrained immorality that finds its exposure in our divorce courts and diminished families, are the legitimate offspring of godless education." —**R. Gilmour**, "What Shall the Schools Teach?" *The Forum* VI (June 1888): 457

SOCIALISM

"Advocates of school feeding are therefore not disturbed by the cry of "socialism." It is no more socialistic than free education, free textbooks, free pencils, free playgrounds, and medical inspection. It is no more socialistic to heat the child's body internally with food than to heat it externally by warming the air of the schoolroom." —**Lewis Terman**, *The Hygiene of the School Child*, 1914, 114

THE STUDY OF EDUCATION

"The subject which involves all other subjects, and therefore the subject in which the education of every one should culminate, is the Theory and Practice of Education." —**Herbert Spencer**, *Education: Intellectual, Moral, and Physical*, 1860, 164

"Only within recent years, with the growing consciousness of the importance of education as a reconstructive force within human experience, with the clearer perception of its fundamental significance in national as well as individual well-being, with the growth of the scientific spirit which will think of nothing as foreign to its inquiry, with the emergence of the individual as such as worthy of education and education as the universal human interest, has the university, 'the bearer across the centuries of the educational tradition,' issued to itself the command, 'Know thyself,' to come to a conscious realization of its own aims and processes, and enrolled among the humanities the patient, loving, thoughtful study of education as a human institution." — **John MacVannel**, *The College Course in the Principles of Education*, 1906, 7

UNIVERSAL EDUCATION

"Too many of our educational ideals are mediæval in their origin; they take as their model some worn-out conception of culture, or they fix their gaze upon some special calling, forgetting that education is no longer the prerogative of the few professional classes, but has become the just privilege of all classes. If, then, we are in earnest about universal education, we must abandon these one-sided ideals, and, once for all, recognize that our education succeeds just to the extent that we make it focus upon the real activities of life." —**Charles DeGarmo**, *Herbart and the Herbartians*, 1895, 241

THE WEAKNESS OF PROGRESSIVE EDUCATION

"I think we find the fundamental weakness, not only of Progressive Education, but also of American education generally. Like a baby shaking a rattle, we seem to be utterly content with action, provided it is sufficiently vigorous and noisy. In the last analysis a very large part of American educational thought, inquiry, and experimentation is much ado about nothing. And, if we are permitted to push the analogy of the rattle a bit further, our consecration to motion is encouraged and supported in order to keep us out of mischief. At least we know that so long as we thus busy ourselves we shall not incur the serious displeasure of our social elders. The weakness of Progressive Education thus lies in the fact that it has elaborated no theory of social welfare, unless it be that of anarchy or extreme individualism." —**George Counts**, *Dare the School Build a New Social Order?* 1932, 6–7

WHAT KNOWLEDGE IS OF MOST WORTH?

"Thus to the question with which we set out—What knowledge is of most worth?—the uniform reply is—Science." —**Herbert Spencer**, *Education: Intellectual, Moral, and Physical*, 1860, 89

"Aristippus, the Greek philosopher, in answer to the question, 'What should the child be taught?' replied, 'A child should be taught those things that he will need to know when he is a man.' This is a fundamental principle. The schools should prepare for life. It remained, however, for the modern world under the leadership of Rousseau, Pestalozzi, and Dewey, to arrive at a conclusion equally fundamental: 'The school is life.' That is to say, the schools must prepare for life in terms of childhood, in terms of interests and motives which dominate child life. In other words, the only content which should be allowed in the course of study is that which has a definite meaning for the children while they are studying it, and which will probably be serviceable to them in their mature years. No other content is worth the time spent on its mastery. Moreover, the omission of the obsolete material leaves room for new and vital material which is visibly useful and therefore easily motivated." —**H. B. Wilson and G. M. Wilson**, *The Motivation of School Work*, 1921, 244–45

Chapter Seven

Exceptional Children

As the schools adopted democratic practices the special education child was to be included in the classroom. There was a call for the development of teacher preparation programs that would enable teachers of special children to provide a quality education. There were discussions about curriculum and school facilities that would be appropriate for children of different abilities. But there was no question that democratic schools were to receive all children regardless of ability or handicap.

Unfortunately, the language used to describe exceptional children and academically slow students will be offensive to modern readers. Slow students were referred to as "defectives," and "retarded" was coming into usage as the modern way to describe special education students. Words like "stupid," "feeble-minded," and "backward" will make twenty-first century readers cringe; however, it is important to remember that the vocabulary used in early special education was emerging.

It is encouraging to note that in 1915 McCord favored "exceptional" as a description for children with special needs. Briggs and Findley decried the use of "bonehead classes" and "blockheads" [Grouping] that were common ways to describe school classes for slower students in the first two decades of the twentieth century. It is interesting to see some enlightened attitudes in the following quotes about the potential of children to learn regardless of ability.

BACKWARD CHILDREN

"The backward child is behind somebody or lower than he ought to be in some arbitrary scale, according to someone's judgment. The mere fact that a child is backward is seen immediately as soon as the standard of measurement is stated. Until that is stated backwardness in itself and by itself has practically no significance." —**Arthur Holmes**, *Backward Children*, 1915, 13–14

EXCEPTIONAL CHILDREN

"The term 'exceptional' was at first used to designate the unusually able or brilliant child. Now we speak of this type of child as 'gifted,' and the term 'exceptional' has lost definition and has become a general heading under which are grouped a variety of classes and subclasses, composed of children bearing almost any defect or suffering from almost any disease or environmental handicap that unfits them for routine school work under conditions provide for the average, normal pupil." —**Clinton P. McCord**, "Medical Supervision and the Exceptional Child," in Louis Rapeer (ed.), *Educational Hygiene, from the Pre-School Period to the University*, 1915, 295–96

GIFTED EDUCATION

"[W]e have been slow to recognize that the pupils of every schoolroom in our graded system, though of the same chronological age, differ widely in inherited capacity to do intellectual work. We are indebted to Terman for a classification which tells us that 20 per cent of all children are of superior mental ability, while 6 per cent are *very* superior. This latter is the group which is provisionally considered under the title 'gifted children.'" —**Henry Herbert Goddard**, "The Gifted Child," *Journal of Educational Sociology* 6 (February 1933): 354–55

HEREDITY

"The supreme fact that permanent backwardness is chiefly due to mental defects of parents seems to be established beyond doubt and continual researches tend to raise the percentages of cases caused by them. The percentages vary from about sixty-six and two thirds per cent. That is, some authors suggest that two-thirds at least of all the feeble-mindedness in the world could be eliminated in a few generations by proper public sentiment and sufficient legislation adequately enforced to prevent the propagation of the mentally unfit. Some insist that nearly all of it would disappear." —**Arthur Holmes**, *Backward Children*, 1915, 168

RETARDED CHILDREN

"A considerable proportion of the retarded children that clog the machinery of most city school systems without doubt owe their backwardness to school curricula and teaching methods that are not in accord with the abilities of these children that will usually be found to be motor-minded. Proper child classification should be the first step toward the correction of these conditions." —**Clinton P. McCord**, "Medical Supervision and the Exceptional Child," in Louis Rapeer (ed.), *Educational Hygiene, from the Pre-School Period to the University*, 1915, 302

RIGHTS OF SPECIAL EDUCATION STUDENTS

"It has been common to provide by law for . . . defective children whose parents are unable to support them. Provision is made either by sending them to private schools at public expense, if necessary, or by establishing special state schools, or by sending to other states and paying for the service. In some states payment is required from those who have financial ability, while the indigent are taught and boarded free. Cities sometimes establish separate rooms and departments of their schools for the blind and deaf mutes." — **Charles Richmond Henderson**, *Introduction to the Study of the Dependent, Defective, and Delinquent Classes*, 1901, 170

SLOW CHILDREN

"Children who are simply slow to understand and backward in learning, but sound in brain, should not be classed with dependents, although they require special methods of teaching in public schools and separate instruction. Many can be taught to work, through sloyd and manual training methods, who profit little by learning to read and write, and who even forget the arts of reading and writing. Rural life is far more favorable for them than rapid, exciting, and stimulating city life; and parents are wise who train such children, as early as possible, for horticultural or agricultural pursuits." — **Charles Richmond Henderson**, *Introduction to the Study of the Dependent, Defective, and Delinquent Classes*, 1901, 182

Chapter 7
SPECIAL EDUCATION

"Special departments are needed in the public schools for the training of that large class of slow and partly defective children, –the blind, the deaf, the stubborn, –who cannot profit by ordinary class work, and who are sorely tempted to play truant and escape from the agony of hopeless struggle in competition with normal children. Many of these do not need to be sent away from home to state schools, but should be taught by special teachers, and permitted to grow up at home and in natural settings." —**Charles Richmond Henderson**, *Introduction to the Study of the Dependent, Defective, and Delinquent Classes*, 1901, 101–2

"The first class ever organized for the deliberate teaching of mental defectives was taught by Seguin in 1837. For decades afterward such instruction was limited to institutions and [was] unknown to the public schools. Sporadic classes occurred earlier, but the real movement for special classes in the public schools did not begin until the nineties of the last century. A score of years would nearly cover their history in this country. The field is hardly more than touched; the methods are experimental; invention and ingenuity have the widest latitude and the most promising opportunities in this educational realm." —**Arthur Holmes**, *Backward Children*, 1915, 221–22

"The special school is of comparatively recent origin, having developed as special schools during the last thirty years. The main function of these schools dealing with delinquents, mental and physical deficients, and retarded children is to discover their possible abilities which are more or less neglected in the regular organization. Psychiatric treatment following psychological examination and the visiting-nurse activities often do more than the regular classroom teacher has either time or talent to accomplish. Maladjustments are remedied, special treatment of individual cases takes place, the child is studied as an individual first rather than wholly as a member of the group, special abilities are discovered and developed, and the child is saved the embarrassment and annoyance of being 'out of his element.' Due to the increased amount of individual attention required of the teacher the enrollment in special classes is usually limited to about fifteen. This calls for a specially trained teacher, a special type of room and equipment, and usually separation from the regular school is desirable, although on that point there seems to be quite a division of opinion." —**Ned Dearborn**, *An Introduction to Teaching*, 1925, 86

"A majority of physically and mentally handicapped children possess aptitudes and abilities which, when developed by proper social, academic, and vocational training can make these children socially and economically competent. To every child we owe the opportunity to develop to the maximum of his capacity. It is our particular duty to see that physically or mentally handicapped children have this opportunity, as a matter of right and fair play, in order to conserve human resources and to afford protection against dependency, pauperism, frustration, and delinquency. The waste of ability involved in our present laissez faire policy warrants our putting forth every effort in behalf of physically and mentally handicapped children, and demands that we supply such facilities that they may have a thorough preparation for community life. The most immediate objective in dealing with the handicapped children is the determination of their numbers, the discovery of the extent to which their needs are being met, and of the facilities necessary to meet their needs." —**William Ellis**, "Physically and Mentally Handicapped Children: A Program for Their Adjustment," *Journal of Educational Sociology* 5 (February 1932): 368–69

"The development of a carefully coördinated program of special educational services for the physically and mentally handicapped children requires unusually competent leadership. It is one of the great undeveloped fields in American education. The program presents many difficult administrative problems in connection with the financing and development of the many unusual services which are essential. Furthermore, it is very desirable to have the active and coördinated coöperation of the large number of organizations in any State—social, medical, civic, welfare, health, service, and fraternal, that are interested in the physical care, education, and general welfare of the handicapped children. Many of these organizations are in a position to offer financial assistance as well as specialized services in the development of the program. The extent to which a State or community meets this baffling problem will be dependent, to a large measure, upon the competency of the leadership provided. Many large cities are also in a position to employ persons unusually well qualified to administer the work." —**Lewis Wilson**, "Organization and Administration of Special Education in the Public Schools," *Journal of Educational Sociology* 6 (February 1933), 379

SPECIAL EDUCATION INSTRUCTION

"The method of instruction does not differ in essential principles from the best methods used with normal children. The process is more slow; the steps must be more carefully analyzed; more use must be made of tangible objects; there must be more repetition of exercises. But all the principles of the best teaching, especially in kindergarten and manual training schools, are essential in these schools. Indeed, a year or more spent in a school of defective children would be an excellent kind of preparation for teaching normal children." —**Charles Richmond Henderson**, *Introduction to the Study of the Dependent, Defective, and Delinquent Classes*, 1901, 180

Chapter 7
STUPID PUPILS

"[T]he teacher is not entitled to assume stupidity or even dullness merely because of irresponsiveness to school subjects or to a lesson as presented by text-book or teacher. The pupil labeled hopeless may react in quick and lively fashion when the thing-in-hand seems to him worth while, as some out-of-school sport or social affair. Indeed, the school subject might move him, were it set in a different context and treated by a different method. A boy dull in geometry may prove quick enough when he takes up the subject in connection with manual training; the girl who seems inaccessible to historical facts may respond promptly when it is a question of judging the character and deeds of people of her acquaintance or of fiction. Barring physical defect or disease, slowness and dullness in *all* directions are comparatively rare." —**John Dewey**, *How We Think*, 1910, 35

"The stupid pupils . . . seldom advance beyond the intermediate grades; hence the grammar or high school teacher is, as a rule, not called upon to deal with them." —**Charles Holley**, *The Teacher's Technique*, 1924, 31

Chapter Eight

Learning

Developing alongside education was the new field of educational psychology. Educational psychology attempted to shed light on how students learned. The key to student achievement was to help teachers understand the relationship between teaching and learning. Teachers understood more about how to teach than they did about how students learned.

Much of what was written about learning was based on personal observation and deduction. For many, the brain was viewed as a kind of muscle that easily tired or became fatigued with schoolwork. Phrenology, a nineteenth century leftover, still provided a key to understanding learning capacity.

However, there were also observations that new learning had to be associated with previous learning and that children needed to construct their own understandings of reality. It was understood that children needed to experience success to learn, and learning was more effective when it came from the need to know rather than from a detailed prescribed curriculum.

Observations of how children learn laid the foundations for what modern educators call learning styles. There were also concerns about how to encourage life-long learning and how to teach higher order thinking skills.

ABILITY

"Pupils will differ in their ability in the same subject. A pupil who is good in division, is not necessarily good in addition or multiplication. One good in grammar or composition may be found weak in spelling or reading. We should not strive, therefore, to do the impossible, to level all differences, and to create an equal interest in all the subjects in all pupils. The most we can do is ask for minimum requirements in such subjects as are required by society at large, and to allow the pupils to develop their natural talents along special lines." —**Felix Arnold**, *Attention and Interest: A Study in Psychology and Education*, 1910, 262

ACQUISITION OF KNOWLEDGE

"To find out how to make knowledge when it is needed is the true end of the acquisition of information in school, not the information itself." —**John and Evelyn Dewey**, *Schools of To-morrow*, 1915, 16

ADULT MODELS

"It is significant how much more trouble some parents and teachers have with the studies of their children or pupils than others. Sometimes the familiar tone of the home, or it may be of the school itself, tends to engender whims and notions in the heads of pupils. Sometimes the direct suggestion comes from parent or teacher that the child will not find such or such a study interesting, or that he cannot master it, when in fact he has made no real effort to find it interesting or master it. In strong confirmation of this view is the fact that the studies in which pupils take little interest are likely to be those in which their teachers take little interest, while their favorite studies are also likely to be the favorite studies of their teachers. These facts are no doubt due in part to the quality of the teaching, but by no means wholly so. Broadly speaking, the question how far the school is itself the parent of its own difficulties, is curious one." —**B. A. Hinsdale**, *The Art of Study: A Manual for Teachers and Students of the Science and the Art of Teaching*, 1900, 134–35

BRAIN-BASED LEARNING

"While modern experimentation has shown that there was something, after all, in phrenology, it has so far failed to do more than establish the general conclusion that the front of the cerebrum is the seat of the thought power, and that intelligence is to some extent proportional to the weight of the brain and the convolutions of its surface." —**Ruric Roark**, *Psychology in Education*, 1895, 30

Learning 77

BRAIN FATIGUE

"[A]void brain fatigue, particularly before it is to be subjected to any trial of memory. In fatigue the brain cells may shrink to half their normal size, and in this condition our associations are fewer in quantity, poorer in quality, slower in revival, and incoherent as related to each other. Any one who has sat up half the night preparing for an examination the next will recognize this description. It is as though the tortoise had withdrawn into its shell and consequently is unable to make connections with the outside world. Though avoiding brain fatigue, it may be observed that moderate intellectual exercise keeps up the one of the brain and is better than disuse for the associative process. A good memory, a good working brain, not so much demands infrequent long vacations as frequent short ones, of which the nightly sleep is the best evidence and illustration." —**Herman Herrell Horne**, *The Psychological Principles of Education*, 1909, 123–24

COGNITIVE FIELD THEORY

"We are . . . concerned to ascertain how the mind naturally and spontaneously assimilates and arranges its acquisitions so that they be surely and readily reproduced. By an appeal to consciousness, we discover that the elements of our knowledge, the various things which have been successively learned, do not remain separate and distinct in the mind, but have in some way become united into an orderly, well-arranged, compact whole. Every new acquisition has entered into a union with previous acquisitions, has been modified by them and assimilated to them. Sometimes it has happened that the new has modified the old in entering into union with it; new facts have compelled old ones to assume new forms, to take on different aspects, to submit to more or less of modification in various directions." —**Daniel Putnam**, *A Manual of Pedagogics*, 1899, 135

CONSTRUCTIVISM

"Thus, the child gradually constructs his world. It is an inner world, at first vague, undifferentiated, then gradually merging from the mists into definiteness. How closely it corresponds to the outer world we cannot discover as easily as we should like, since at first the impressions constituting the inner life are inadequately expressed. . . . Much of our quibbling over courses of study is the result of a blind effort to make the child construct mentally his whole environment. So-called instruction on our part may mean very little to the child." —**Harriet Scott**, *Organic Education*, 1899, 340

CRAMMING

"The question as to the value of cramming has often raised and variously answered. Much depends upon the meaning given to the term. If by it is meant a final general review of what has previously been intelligently learned, with the purpose of refreshing old associations, its value is real and great. However, cramming is usually taken to mean a hurried attempt to learn in a few hours what should have occupied weeks in mastering. As thus interpreted, cramming is a violation of almost every principle we have just enunciated." —**Herbert Foster**, *Principles of Teaching in Secondary Education*, 1921, 93–94

DETERMINING SUCCESS IN THE CLASSROOM

"There are two factors in teaching, the teacher and the pupil, and the essential factor is the pupil. It is what the pupil does, not what the teacher says, that determines the success of the teaching process." —**Emerson E. White**, *The Art of Teaching: A Manual*, 1901, 34

DETRIMENTS TO HIGHER ORDER THINKING SKILLS

"It is believed that arrested development of the higher mental and moral faculties is caused in many cases by the school. The habit of teaching with too much thoroughness and too long-continued drill the semi-mechanical branches of study, such as arithmetic, spelling, the discrimination of colours, the observation of surface and solid forms, and even the distinctions of formal grammar, often leaves the pupil fixed in the lower stages of growth and unable to exercise the higher functions of thought." —**William Torrey Harris**, *Psychologic Foundations of Education*, 1898, 6–7

THE EFFECTS OF FAILURE

"We have seen that a large part of all the children in our public schools fail to make normal progress. They fail repeatedly. They are thoroughly trained in failure. The effect of such training should be carefully considered, for the problem it presents is a grave one. It does not make much difference what we have to do, whether it is a great thing or a little thing, so long as we feel that it is possible for us and that we can do it if we try. There are few more hopeless things in the world than to have it borne in upon us that we are driving against a thing we cannot do. Yet this is the sort of training that we are giving a large part of all our children." —**Leonard Ayres**, *Laggards in Our Schools*, 1909, 220

FATIGUE

"The amount of study or muscular exercise which produces simply normal fatigue in a healthy child may produce abnormal fatigue in a child who is physically below par; and if this amount of work is continued the child must have a nervous collapse, or nervous prostration. Children that are the offspring of alcoholic or neurotic parents, those that are anaemic, those that have defects of sight or hearing, those that are growing very rapidly, and especially young girls who are just entering the period of adolescence, are very susceptible to nervous collapse from overwork. Overpressure in schools is most apt to show itself in springtime, after the long winter, when children have had little outdoor exercise. During this period of the year, moreover, increase in height is more rapid; this always causes great strain on the blood-making organs, and so predisposes to anaemia and hence to nervous exhaustion. Mouth breathers and those children who have adenoid growths in the throat are also more liable than others to anaemia and abnormal fatigue." —**Thomas J. McEvoy**, *The Science of Education*, 1911, 131–32

"Young pupils cannot, as a rule, work uninterruptedly so long as can older pupils and adults. School children should, however, be encouraged to keep at their study over a considerable period, and not think that because they have worked fifteen minutes or even an hour it is time to quit. We often get the idea that we have worked long enough, and then we begin to feel fatigued. There is little danger of the normal child seriously overworking in school. Authorities are at present of the opinion that dangerous fatigue among American school children is rare." —**Stephen Colvin and William Chandler Bagley**, *Human Behavior: A First Book in Psychology for Teachers*, 1921, 65

Chapter 8

I HAVE GONE

"Every teacher is familiar with the story of the boy who wrote, 'I have gone,' on a piece of paper fifty times, in order to impress the correct form on his mind, and then on the bottom of the page left a note for the teacher beginning, 'I have went home.'" —**John and Evelyn Dewey**, *Schools of Tomorrow*, 1915, 84

LEARNING

"All now agree that the mind can learn only what is related to other things learned before, and that we must start from the knowledge that the children really have and develop this as germs, otherwise we are showing objects that require close scrutiny only to indirect vision, or talking to the blind about color. Alas for the teacher who does not learn more from his children than he can ever hope to teach them! Just in proportion as teachers do this do they cease to be merely mechanical, and acquire interest, perhaps enthusiasm, and surely an all-compensating sense of growth in their work and life." —**G. Stanley Hall**, *The Contents of Children's Minds*, 1907, 22–23

"The desire to know for the sake of understanding has practically died out in this land, probably because the schools do little if anything to foster it. From the primary school to the university almost everything is *traditional*; learning is prepared in formal doses, and it must be taken just as prescribed. The instructor hands out the doses, in the text-books or the lectures, and the pupils raise no queries nor make any objections." —**M. V. O'Shea**, *Social Development and Education*, 1909, 237

"Many books have been written on methods of teaching, but comparatively little has been said about methods of learning. While this was quite natural in view of our scant knowledge of child psychology, it has had the unfortunate effect of overemphasizing the arrangement and form of lesson plans. The method of lesson-presentation has been settled chiefly by reference to the subject-matter, and too often with inadequate comprehension by the teacher of the wider meaning of the facts which it contained. The logical arrangement of the parts of the topic for study and the importance from the teacher's view-point, of each portion of the whole, have determined the lesson's plan. But in acquiring knowledge, the logical arrangement is not always the pedagogical." —**Edgar James Swift**, *Learning and Doing*, 1914, 100

"The teacher who thinks that she can get satisfactory results merely by compelling children to repeat over and over again the particular form to be mastered is doomed to disappointment. Indeed, it is not infrequently true that the dislike which children get for the dreary exercises which have little or no meaning for them interferes to such a degree with the formation of the habit we hope to secure as to develop a maximum of inaccuracies rather than any considerable improvement." —**George Strayer and Naomi Norsworthy**, *How to Teach*, 1922, 67–68

"In our school work we have ceased to think the most valuable thing we can do for the child is stuffing him with information. We have come to think that, even in the purely informational subjects, much of the material dealt with is not intended for permanent retention. It is mere water that makes the mill-wheel turn, and then passes on forever useless after it has done its work." —**Martin J. Stormzand**, *Progressive Methods of Teaching*, 1924, 84

LEARNING BY DOING

"No power of the mind is developed and trained except by fitting exercise. In order to secure such exercise, means and opportunities must be supplied. The senses can be trained by giving them something to do. The eye learns to see by seeing; the ear by hearing; and the other senses become skillful in their peculiar work by doing it…. It is the teacher's business to give the proper instruction, direction, and guidance. So much being granted, the maxim of Comenius is true: '*Let things that have to be done be learned by doing them.*'" —**Daniel Putnam**, *A Manual of Pedagogics*, 1899, 162

LEARNING CURVES

"Ebbinghaus [found that] a person retains approximately two-thirds of what he learned after 20 minutes, one-half after an hour, one-third after nine hours, and but one-fourth after two days. . . . *We forget very rapidly at first and then more and more slowly.*" —**Edward Long Jr.**, *Introductory Psychology for Teachers*, 1922, 91–92

LEARNING STYLES

"Some pupils are predominately visualizers, others audiles, and still others motiles. This is very well illustrated in spelling. Some children remember spelling best by looking at the words. They have a visual picture of the letters. Others remember best the sound of the letters. Still others remember the correct spelling only after writing it out or after spelling it to themselves, thus getting the muscular feel in the hand or in the vocal cords." —**W. W. Charters**, *Methods of Teaching*, 1912, 122–23

"Once she has found what a pupil is primarily and most constantly interested in, the teacher is ready for next question, 'How does he learn—by eye, ear, or hand?' Some children learn chiefly through their eyes and are called visual types. They must see a thing and then they recall the picture of it in their minds. Others learn by ear, or are auditory types. They must be told and recall what they remember by hearing it. Some are kinesthetic or motor types. They seize upon their knowledge chiefly with their hands and store it up in their muscles and motor-nervous mechanism. Absolutely pure types of any one of the three enumerated are almost never found." —**Arthur Holmes**, *Backward Children*, 1915, 205–6

"The average man learns in many ways at once. There are four varieties of exceptional people, however, whose nervous systems are specially adapted to particular ways and singularly poor in others. These varieties are the eye learner, the ear learner, the throat-and-tongue learner, and the manipulative learner." —**Walter Pitkin**, *The Art of Learning*, 1931, 86

LIFE-LONG LEARNERS

"The great purpose of modern teachers is to emancipate the pupil, *i.e.*, to help the pupil to help himself more and more until he needs no more help from others in his own development. The pupil must therefore be put into the best possible physical condition, obstructions which are really insurmountable to him must be removed, he must learn to think by means of books and how to use his mental capabilities, and in the crisis of his natural development his personality must be shaped by superior personality." —**Charles C. Boyer**, *Modern Methods for Teachers*, 1908, 78

"[I]t has been pointed out that, in the United States, only ten per cent of our adult population have had a high school education, while only 50 per cent have ever completed the grammar grades. The impression that when a child leaves the jurisdiction of the school system his education is complete, is a common fallacy that must be eradicated. The citizenry of America must set the example for the world by making education not only the chief aim of the first few years of their lives but during their entire allotted period of life." —**George Strayer and N. L. Engelhardt**, *The Classroom Teacher at Work in American Schools*, 1920, 381–82

MEMORY

"When memory shall take its proper place and our pupils be taught to observe, to think, to do, instead of to memorize and repeat, then will the growth of our pupils compel the respect of the wise for our schools, and the fruit of the tree of knowledge be for the sustenance and health of the people." —**George Howland**, *Practical Hints for the Teachers of Public Schools*, 1899, 53

NEED TO KNOW AS THE BASIS OF LEARNING

"Adult society has always felt the need of transmitting to its young, its own body of knowledge, skill, and culture; but it has often been guilty of trying to force upon children a view of life to which there was no answering sense of need—no basis in interest; and often, too, this foreign view of life has been presented from its form side with no effort to acquaint children with its content. It is true that children should grow into men and women, but it is no more true that they become men and women by gaining the vocabulary of adults than it is that a little girl of eight in a long skirt is a woman. What is taught, then, must answer to a sense of need (native or acquired)." —**J. A. H. Keith**, *Elementary Education: Its Problems and Processes*, 1905, 259

"Why should children be expected to understand the importance of knowledge when the need for it has not yet arisen? One of the conditions of the teacher is to produce situations in which this need will be a recurring factor, and the conditions that meet this educational requirement are those in which the children are the planners and the workers. In short, they are situations of action." —**Edgar James Swift**, *Learning and Doing*, 1914, 32

"The assignment of school tasks is often very much like requiring one to eat when one is not hungry. There is no genuine satisfaction in such work because it is not done in response to any real feeling of need for it. The attitude in performing these tasks is either that of conventional tolerance or sometimes even poorly concealed hostility." —**Frederick Bonser**, *The Elementary School Curriculum*, 1922, 22

TAXONOMY OF OBJECTIVES FOR THINKING

"The intellectual acts of which the mind is capable, classified on the basis of the 'stuff' upon which the mind can make attacks in thinking, *i.e.*, in arriving at ideas and relating them, are as follows: (1) perception, the act of thinking the sensible present, as in looking at a rose, (2) memory, the act of thinking the past again, as in recognizing faces, (3) imagination, the act of thinking combinations that merely resemble sensible experience, as in reading novels or in dreaming, (4) judgment, the act of thinking likeness or unlikeness by direct comparison, as estimating length or weight by sight, (5) reasoning, the act of thinking relations and their consequences, as in arguments that end in the discovery of causes, laws, and effects, and (6) self-consciousness, the act of thinking the present experiences of the mind as self." —**Charles C. Boyer**, *Modern Methods for Teachers*, 1908, 24–25

Chapter Nine

Motivating Students

Motivation of students has been a perennial issue with teachers. Finding ways to interest students and capture their attention is often at the heart of effective teaching.

Some writers felt that the search for ways to interest students could become a constant struggle as students became more and more immune to attention getting devices. Parker suggested that regardless of how interesting a lesson might be the teacher should remember that children had shorter attention spans than adults.

No matter how teachers valued student attention, the real work in the classroom was the delivery of content. Teachers were advised to be certain that the material to be learned was not set too far above the students' ability to understand, that subject matter must have relevance to the daily lives of students, and they should capitalize on student interests.

When it came to motivating students, William James, perhaps the most preeminent psychologists of the day recommended that "The teacher pounce upon the most listless child and wake him up." Contrary to modern thought, Colvin and Bagley felt that the sting of punishment could motivate students to work harder. However, most writers believed that true motivation occurred when teachers were able to connect the lessons of the classroom with life in the world outside the school.

ATTENTION AND INATTENTION

"The enlightened teacher, will . . . in a systematic manner, cultivate relaxation in her pupils. She will take a constructive and not a sensitive attitude toward inattention. Much of the school's inattention is attention to something else, but in young children there are many periods of reflex, instinctive brown study, in which the attention is diffused, dispersed,–momentary cat naps. These have a biological, hygienic import, and ought to be cultivated rather than combated. If teachers had absolute sway over the attention of children, too many would become priggish little adults." —**Arnold Gesell and Beatrice Gesell**, *The Normal Child and Primary Education*, 1912, 77

ATTENTION SPAN OF CHILDREN

"The teacher who really strives to develop pure acts of attention on the part of the child should remember that no matter what the object of attention may be, how strong the motive which prompts the interest, or how delightful at first the mental act, exhaustion sets in with children very quickly." —**Francis Parker**, *Talks on Pedagogics*, 1894, 134

BOREDOM

"[T]he greater problem is the weariness, not of exhausted but of unapplied resources. It is the boredness which causes children to throw aside their work from sheer lack of interest in it, and to feel that the lack of interest is a legitimate excuse for their neglect of it. It is unfortunate that there has grown up with the Doctrine of Interest, a mischievous heresy which accepts just this excuse. Teachers who allow such excuses to stand, do so at a sacrifice of character as well as of work quality. All good work is interesting. Find the interest, hunt it out—but if it eludes pursuit, *the work is still to be done*." —**Frances Morehouse**, *The Discipline of the School*, 1914, 227

DEVELOPING COOPERATION AND INTEREST

"The teacher with whom the pupils coöperate most cheerfully is he who can readily select aspects of the subject matter that are directly appealing. There are various ways by which teachers can develop this skill. Care in collecting effective illustrations, patience in finding applications that are familiar to pupils, and willingness to let pupils develop their own approaches that may seem irrelevant, are all useful. Too few teachers conscientiously undertake to 'sell' their subjects. Few pupils can recognize values for high-school subjects that are not made explicit and convincing through skillful demonstration and illustration in terms of everyday life." —**Douglas Waples**, *Problems in Classroom Method*, 1929, 175

ENCOURAGEMENT

"Children need encouragement as much as adults need it. A teacher known to the writer recently secured a transfer from a certain school because her principal had the peculiarity of always picking out the flaws in her work and never praising the part that had no flaws. Hundreds of children suffer the same kind of thoughtless criticism. Their teachers find fault with all their imperfections, but never encourage them by praise when they do well." —**Joseph S. Taylor**, *Art of Class Management and Discipline*, 1903, 35

THE FUNDAMENTAL DIFFICULTY

"The fundamental difficulty is that the work in which the schools seek to engage the child is not significant to him. It does not satisfy the needs which the individual child experiences. It does not gratify any hunger or yearning he has felt. It does not answer any questions which his experiences have raised in his mind. It does not contribute to the solution of any problems which he has encountered in actual life. With the work thus external and foreign to the child's personal hungers, longings, questions, experiences, and problems, it does not render him aggressively self-active. In the average school, we find him listlessly sitting, looking, listening, and answering when questioned, rather than initiating, doing, and creating. Yet we know definitely that growth and mastery can come to the child only as a result of vigorous, aggressive self-activity." —**H. B. Wilson and G. M. Wilson**, *The Motivation of School Work*, 1921, 10

INTEREST AND ATTENTION

"The teacher who constantly caters to the pupils' love of the spectacular must go to greater and greater lengths if he would attract the attention of his pupils, and the time must come, sooner or later, when his *blasé* charges will be bored even by matters of legitimate interest." —**William Chandler Bagley**, *Classroom Management*, 1911, 154

"The lack of practical interest in high school work is too often intensified by a lack of vitality in teaching, from which the college preparatory student suffers as much as the boy destined for industry. In the same spirit which omits practical branches from the curriculum, the instructor often fails to make constantly the connection between what is taught in school and the actual facts of the children's experience. History gets to be a world shut in between the covers of a book. Physiology and hygiene are something to recite about and not to apply to the ventilation of one's bedroom. Mathematics becomes an abstract juggling with figures. Even literature, that hardest of subjects to kill, falls into the category of things to be learned and not lived, and, instead of opening their eyes to the undreamt wonder of the world, succeeds merely in giving children a positive distaste for books." —**Ruth Mary Weeks**, *The People's School: A Study in Vocational Training*, 1912, 35–36

"Educationally, it then follows that to attach importance to interest means to attach some feature of seductiveness to material otherwise indifferent; to secure attention and effort by offering a bribe of pleasure. This procedure is properly stigmatized as 'soft' pedagogy; as a 'soup-kitchen' theory of education." —**John Dewey**, *Democracy and Education*, 1916, 148–49

"Many a child has quit school before completing the course of study, not because he was compelled to stay out to work, but because interest failed, owing to the lack of connection between his school work and his outside interests and activities. Many others have continued in school until they have obtained a smattering of what it had to teach, and later found little immediate use for what they had learned." —**George Betts and Otis Hall**, *Better Rural Schools*, 1914, 61–62

"If the child's interests lag, make vivid the object that he is to attend to, and his wandering thoughts will return to their proper place. Emphasize, repeat, reiterate, and gradually the desired attention will be called forth. If the lesson is dragging, do something to awaken interest, even if it is nothing more than to go to the blackboard and draw a diagram. Better still, get the pupils to do something, for there is always interest in self-activity. Facts cast in the form of verse are often more easily learned than when presented without such aid. A painful experience is sometimes the only thing to impress the dull mind. It has been found in studying the behavior of animals that they learn more quickly by being punished for failures than by being rewarded for successes. The rat that is learning to thread his way to the center of the maze will get there more quickly, if he is given an electric shock every time he enters a blind alley than if the stimulus of the food solely is relied on. What is true of the animal is probably to an extent true if the child. That is to say, education cannot entirely dispense with pain as a stimulus." —**Stephen Colvin and William Chandler Bagley**, *Human Behavior: A First Book in Psychology for Teachers*, 1921, 59–60

"Boys and girls do their best work only when they concentrate their attention upon the work to be done. One of the greatest fallacies that has ever crept into our educational thought is that which suggests that there is great value in having people work in fields in which they are not interested, and in which they do not freely give their attention. Any one who is familiar with children, or with grown-ups, must know that it is only when interest is at a maximum that the effort put forth approaches the limit of capacity set by the individual's ability." —**George Strayer and Naomi Norsworthy**, *How to Teach*, 1922, 49

"School work is often lacking in interest just because a scholastic or academic tendency to intellectual aloofness, or pursuing knowledge for its own sake and avoiding any contact with the 'sordid affairs of practical life.'" —**Claude Crawford**, *The Technique of Study*, 1928, 165–66

MOTIVATION

"People sometimes say, 'I should like to teach if only pupils cared to learn.' But then there would be little need of teaching. Boys who have made up their minds that knowledge is worth while are pretty sure to get it, without regard to teachers. Our chief concern is with those who are unawakened. In the Sistine Chapel Michael Angelo has depicted the Almighty moving in clouds over the rugged earth where lies the newly created Adam, hardly aware of himself. The tips of the fingers touch, the Lord's and Adam's, and the huge frame loses its inertness and rears itself into action. Such may be the electrifying touch of the teacher." —**George Herbert Palmer**, *The Ideal Teacher*, 1908, 22–23

"The teacher must pounce upon the most listless child and wake him up." —**William James**, *Talks to Teachers*, 1910, 105

"The law of motivation deducible from the illustrations given may be stated as follows: *To motivate school work it is necessary only to give it vital connection with the pupils' present interests*. This law may be taken as a fundamental principle for guidance in all teaching." —**H. B. Wilson and G. M. Wilson**, *The Motivation of School Work*, 1921, 53–54

"Motivation is 'the stimulation of a desire upon the part of the learner to master the subject presented.'" —**H. W. Nutt**, *Principles of Teaching High School Pupils*, 1922, 109, quoted by William Kilpatrick in *Source Book in the Philosophy of Education*, 1934, 424

Chapter Ten

Parents

Parents were urged to take a more active role in the education of their children. On one hand, schools became aware of the influence of parents and home life had on the success of students. On the other hand, schools had to cope with angry parents.

Dealing with angry parents is not a new issue for schools. The unsatisfied parent who threatens to "go downtown" to report the school to a higher authority was around at the turn of the last century and is still with us today. Pickard questioned the value of the school standing *in loco parentis*. Other writers wondered if some parents expected too much from teachers and the schools.

ANGRY PARENTS

"All interviews of a controversial nature between parent and teacher should be held in the office of the principal. No parent should be permitted to interview a teacher at her class room, and notice to this effect should be conspicuously posted in the hallways, and teachers trained to refuse to enter upon such an interview." —**Arthur C. Perry Jr.**, *The Management of a City School*, 1908, 51

"In spite of the utmost endeavor on the part of the principal and teachers to present fairly the side of the school, occasionally an unreasonable parent remains unconvinced. His departure is made with the time-honored threat to 'go higher' or to 'report you to the Board of Education' or 'to the Superintendent.'" —**Arthur C. Perry Jr.**, *The Management of a City School*, 1908, 52–53

"Many of the complaints which come to a principal at his office he should handle and settle without saying anything to the teacher about them. If the teacher is right, as she usually is, he should protect her from the annoyance and worry incident to the complaint. It is part of the principal's business to shield his teachers as much as possible that they may do their teaching in peace and under the most favorable conditions." —**Elwood P. Cubberley**, *The Principal and His School*, 1923, 298

BAD HOME CONDITIONS

"Bad home conditions are . . . [a] cause of disciplinary troubles. If the children are not taught and controlled at home, it will show in their school conduct. Parents often permit their children to flout their authority, to speak disrespectfully, and to use vulgar and profane language. If the home life is not happy, the children may be morose, stubborn, and impudent. If they do not have suitable food and sleep they will be nervous, inattentive, and mischievous. Physical defects, such as bad teeth, diseased tonsils, and malnutrition are inevitable attendants upon poor home conditions, and they inevitably complicate school government with tardiness, irregularity of attendance, irritability, and inability to make progress. Children who labor under these handicaps deserve great sympathy, but they also need special training that will help them to improve their home conditions as they get older." —**John Almack and Albert Lang**, *The Beginning Teacher*, 1928, 114–15

INFLUENCE OF THE HOME

"One cannot with assurance state that the training of the children of preschool age has remained the same. Millions of automobiles take father, mother, and the children out for 'a drive,' and when they return home, it is by no means clear that there is an hour of study, discussion, or devotion before retiring. Yet the influence of the home, centered about the father and mother, leaves its imprint upon the attitudes and habits of each child." —**Ned Dearborn**, *An Introduction to Teaching*, 1925, 111

IN LOCO PARENTIS

"'*In loco parentis*' is a phrase which is doing incalculable harm in shifting burdens from the parent, now too much relieved, upon the public school, already overburdened." —**J. L. Pickard**, *School Supervision*, 1905, 77

PARENTING SKILLS

"If by some strange chance not a vestige of us descended to the remote future save a pile of our school books or some college examination papers, we may imagine how puzzled an antiquary of the period would be in finding in them no indication that the learners were ever likely to be parents. 'This must have been the curriculum for their celibates,' we may fancy him concluding. 'I perceive here an elaborate preparation for many things: especially for reading the books of extinct populations and of co-existing nations (from which indeed it seems clear that these people had very little worth reading in their own tongue), but I find no reference whatever to the bringing up of children. They could not have been so absurd as to omit all training for this gravest of responsibilities. Evidently then, this was the school course of one of their monastic orders.'" —**Herbert Spencer**, *Education: Intellectual, Moral, and Physical*, 1860, 44–45

PARENTS

"[P]arents often expect more of a teacher than he can possibly accomplish. They expect him to advance their children in learning, without making proper allowance for the difference of abilities which his pupils possess. Every parent wishes his son to be foremost in improvement, and he expects it, because he wishes it. At the same time, he expects the school to be a perfect pattern of good order …. He forgets that probably fifty other parents are expecting for their children as much as he for his, and that the teacher is laboring with a laudable ambition to do faithfully all that can be expected of him with some three or four score of individuals whose tempers and capacities and habits are as different as their countenances." —**Robert King**, *School Interests and Duties*, 1894, 23

"[T]he attitude of many parents would indicate that they regard the promotion of their children at the close of the term as an intrinsic return due them for their school-taxes. It is though promotion were a form of vested right which the school, for some mysterious reason, was determined to withhold from the child, and to gain which the parent must struggle with equal determination. It is as though promotion were equivalent to a theatre ticket which the parent had purchased and which a spiteful box-office man was refusing to deliver to him. The fact is that the whole matter of promotion is solely a question as to where in the school the pupil may best be served." — **Arthur C. Perry Jr.**, *The Status of the Teacher*, 1912, 22

"The home often complains that it is not informed of the shortcomings of the children and parents insist that these would have been corrected had they been known. The school, on the other hand, complains, and justly of the general indifference of the home." —**Florence Milner**, *The Teacher*, 1912, 69

"The parent may assume that the teacher will instruct his child intellectually and morally, but he cannot rightfully expect the teacher to devote a widely disproportionate part of her time in coaxing his child to conduct himself in accordance with fully recognized rules of decorum. It is not expected that the parent shall actually take the place of the teacher in the performance of her normal duties; but when the misconduct of the child goes beyond the reach of the ordinary classroom methods of a skillful teacher, it is reasonable to expect the parent to coöperate in securing proper discipline." —**Arthur C. Perry Jr.**, *Discipline as a School Problem*, 1915, 223–24

"In too many instances parents seem to be more anxious to have their children go through school than they are to have the school go through their children." —**Oscar Corson**, *Our Public Schools: Their Teachers, Pupils and Patrons*, 1918, 273

A RETURN TO THE GOOD OLD DAYS

"There are some parents who are so enamored of the school which trained them that they are afraid of the new school which carries boys and girls along faster than pupils used to be carried through the elementary school. Such parents go back in imagination to the golden age of their childhood and fabricate notions about the excellence of those earlier schools which have no basis in fact." —**Charles Judd**, *The Evolution of a Democratic School System*, 1918, 104

Chapter Eleven

Schools

The most dramatic and visual evidence that education was changing came from writing about schools themselves. The schools were becoming modern with facilities that encouraged learning. Rural schools were moving from one-room schools scattered across remote areas to consolidated schools housed in new buildings that could provide many more opportunities for children.

Along with the consolidated school came issues of transportation as the school wagon began to pick up children and deliver them to school. New city schools were being built throughout the country to accommodate increased enrollments. But it was not just the buildings themselves that were new; what was going on inside the buildings was revolutionary. As early as 1893 Joseph Mayer Rice was calling for the end of antiquated schools that taught only facts, as he promoted the modern school that taught children how to think.

There were myriad issues that confronted the schools. Some of the problems faced by the schools were school funding, health and safety problems, critics, and proving the value of a high-school diploma. Perhaps the most lasting changes in the schools were the introduction of the kindergarten, the advancement of the junior high school, and the opening of the high school to all children.

There was a strong call for the establishment of kindergarten. The difficulty with providing universal kindergarten was that states had laws defining the age when children could start school. Most state laws defined the start age at six; other states school began for children at ages seven and eight. Since state funding was connected to the legal definition of school age it was difficult to find ways to finance kindergarten programs. However, kindergarten proponents persisted and most states found ways to include kindergarten in the school program.

Beginning about 1908 states began to create junior highs, and by 1920 the junior high school was, for the most part, a formal, nationally accepted educational division. Benson suggested that junior high school was more than an organization of grades, it was a method of instruction; that is, the junior high became a place for a unique educational program designed for preadolescents.

The high school began to attract more students. Once reserved for the elite who were preparing for the university, the high school was becoming what Betts called "the people's college." However, there were concerns about the undue influence colleges exerted over the developing high school curriculum and what should constitute a proper high school education for girls.

ANTIQUATED SCHOOLS

"By an unscientific or mechanical school is meant one that is still conducted on the antiquated notion that the function of the school consists primarily, if not entirely, in crowding into the memory of the child a certain number of cut-and-dried facts—that is, that the school exists simply for the purpose of giving the child a certain amount of information. As, in such schools, the manner in which the mind acquires ideas is naturally disregarded, it follows that the teachers are held responsible for nothing beyond securing certain memoriter results." —**Joseph Mayer Rice**, *The Public School System of the United States*, 1893, 20

BETTER SCHOOLS

"Some one has said that the race advances on the feet of little children. If the children of our present day can have better conditions under which to develop than did the children of the generation just past, then the race has made a distinct advance. If better habits can be developed in children that now attend our schools, then the race has so far gained over what it received from the schools of the past." —**L. N. Hanes**, "Hygienic School Environment," in Louis Rapeer (ed.), *Educational Hygiene, from the Pre-School Period to the University*, 1915, 312

BLAME FOR POOR SCHOOLWORK

"Every teacher knows how few boys and girls grow up with good habits of study and powers of application. The colleges and universities criticise the preparatory schools for this defect, and the teachers of each grade report that the habit has been acquired and fixed in some lower one. Hence some logical sages lay the blame on the kindergarten system." —**John Mason Tyler**, *Growth and Education*, 1907, 212

"The transition from grammar schools to high schools has been attended by many serious difficulties. Teachers in high schools have gone so far as to make a sweeping condemnation of methods and results in the elementary schools. Pupils entering high schools are said to be deficient in matter, power of oral and written expression, habits of study, capacity for adaptation, and desire for knowledge." —**Thomas J. McEvoy**, *The Science of Education*, 1911, 166

"It is a standing joke among administrators that teachers are pretty sure to blame their failures on some one else. This may be the previous teacher, the parents, the pupils, or, sometimes, the principal. It is not good policy to offer such excuses, and usually they are not authentic. No one person can honestly take all the credit for the good traits shown by a group of children; similarly no one person can be blamed for all their short-comings. A teacher who in September says that her pupils are low in arithmetic because they were not taught well the year before forgets that three or more months have gone by since the close of school, and that in three months children may forget more than half of what they learned during a whole year." —**John Almack and Albert Lang**, *The Beginning Teacher*, 1928, 174

CLASS SIZE

"It is generally agreed . . . that, a normal class membership of 20 to 25, no teacher can hope to give successful secondary instruction with a program of more than 25 class periods per week, and 20 is much better. For teachers of English under present methods even this latter number should be reduced. Beyond 25 periods, quality deteriorates rapidly and gives place to the merest hack work, however well meant." —**W. D. Lewis**, "High School Administration," in Paul Monroe (ed.), *Principles of Secondary Education*, 1914, 183

CLASSROOM SIZE

"The best size for an elementary classroom for about forty pupils seems to be, all matters considered: length 32 feet, height 13 feet, width 24 feet. This size has in consideration sufficient lighting space, the carrying power of voices, distance for seeing and hearing, ease of class management and instruction, ventilation, building economy, etc. The height may be reduced six inches and the length a foot or more, if desired. In high schools the height should be the same, but the floor area and shape must be variable." —**L. W. Rapeer**, "School Sanitation Standards," in Louis Rapeer (ed.), *Educational Hygiene*, 1915, 339

COLLEGE ADMISSION

"To close the door of the university on an aspiring student merely because he has not pursued a prescribed set of required studies, no matter how good as to quantity and quality his pre-collegiate work in other studies has been, is to close the door of the highest educational opportunity a democratic society can command. Fortunately, the universities are gradually adjusting themselves to modern demands in this regard; and it is daily becoming clearer that before many years all universities will admit that any good secondary education, either with or without the classics, is a good preparation for college or university. It is even safe to predict, I think, that before many years it will be clear to all higher institutions of learning that unless they recognize this truth, the main line of progress will lead past instead of through their doors." — **Paul Hanus**, *A Modern School*, 1905, 39

COMMUNICATION AMONG GRADE LEVELS

"[Superintendents] should frankly face the question as to what kind and amount of modification of the content of courses, of the methods of instruction, and of the program for personal control of pupils is desired in both the grammar grades and in the high schools. It is a lamentable condition, and one easily remedied if a superintendent sets himself to the task, that many principals and teachers are to a very small extent informed of the work and of the definite aims of the proximate grades, either above or below." —**Thomas Briggs**, *The Junior High School*, 1920, 13

CRITICS

"[I]t is impossible to test the validity of an educational theory as easily and satisfactorily as that of a medical theory or a theory of jurisprudence, the reason being that the results are so slow in education, and that there are so many supplemental factors to be taken into account. . . . Possibly it is this very difficulty in the way of accurate measurement of educational results that makes so many inexpert critics ready to express their educational convictions. For there is nothing that the average man loves more to do than to publish and defend his own particular educational creed. It therefore comes about that many who would not dare to show their lack of information and grasp in the fields of science or mathematics by writing articles or appearing in public lectures in these fields, rush into print or readily proclaim their educational doctrines with at least as little technical knowledge of the educational factors as they have of science or mathematics. This probably explains why so much of the printed upon educational theory is without value, and no small part of it actually misleading." —**George Herbert Betts**, *Social Principles of Education*, 1912, 251–52

"A great deal of the criticism that the schools meet from business men who employ public-school graduates is due to the fact that—along with the valuable habits that the school has implanted—certain very undesirable modes of behavior have been permitted to become habitual. Sometimes these are represented by clumsy and uneconomical methods of writing and computation; more frequently it is the moral habits that are defective. The boy has not been 'disciplined' into habits of obedience, promptness, industry, and respect for those in authority; and his bad habits must be uprooted before he can his work properly." —**Stephen Colvin and William Chandler Bagley**, *Human Behavior: A First Book in Psychology for Teachers*, 1921, 174

EDUCATION FOR GIRLS

"As a rule, the girls in any community are quite as intelligent as the boys. If we pass from childhood to youth, we still fail to discover any mental inferiority of young women to young men. When the two sexes are educated together, the female performs her task with some apparent ease as the male. Young women acquire languages as readily, comprehend abstruse problems as quickly, and are quite as likely to take prizes in mathematics and other studies, as male students. In adult age we find the same intellectual equality of the sexes. And yet here we may find an excuse for any deficiency on the part of women, by remembering that she has not had the same opportunity for mental development that man has enjoyed." —**D. P. Livermore**, "Women's Mental Status," *The Forum* (March 1888): 93

"It is hard to defend an educational policy that will require a girl to spend several of the best years of her life in the mastery of mathematical processes and formulae which she never employs, and in the acquisition of linguistic inflections and vocabulary of a language she never uses, and then send her into the most crucial and important experiences of her life [homemaking and motherhood] in absolute ignorance of the problems to be confronted." —**George Herbert Betts**, *Social Principles of Education*, 1912, 277

"Of all the subjects in the curriculum, none will be found of greater import in the life of the girl than music and drawing. Any one who looks upon human life from the larger standpoint sees that a vital need of woman is to attain harmonious social adjustment, to become attractive in conduct, in personal appearance, in the capacity to interest people, and provide for their enjoyment in agreeable ways. Drawing and music, taught so as to give pupils an appreciation of harmonies in all the varied situations of real life, and ability to create such harmonies in form and color and sound and general arrangement will prove of great service to any girl, no matter in what places her lines may be cast." —**M. V. O'Shea**, *Everyday Problems of Teachers*, 1912, 334

"Women and girls have grown up under a social system that has assumed on their part fundamentally different tastes and interests from those of men and boys. The social system has sometimes expressed itself in terms which imply inferiority of women as compared with men. It is natural, therefore, that at a period when women and girls are taking a new place in the social scheme, there should be at first a good deal of attention given to the demonstration that women are not inferior to men. The simplest demonstration can, of course, be given by putting girls into the same classes with boys and requiring of them the same intellectual tasks. For some years past the experiment has been under way. Girls have shown themselves not only quite as competent intellectually as boys but in some respects superior." —**Charles Judd**, *Introduction to the Scientific Study of Education*, 1918, 176

ELEMENTARY SCHOOLS

"Pupils fail of promotion in the fourth or fifth grade much more commonly than in the second, third, or sixth. In other words, there is here, just after the primary grades, a period of violent readjustment." —**Charles Judd**, *Introduction to the Scientific Study of Education*, 1918, 175

"Over forty per cent of the total time in [elementary] schools is given to formal instruction in the language arts—reading, language, spelling, and penmanship. If to these subjects is added arithmetic, well over one half of the time is accounted for. Whatever may be the impression to the contrary, the facts speak for themselves: the three R's still dominate the elementary school curriculum. History and science receive but little attention, and music and art are given only perfunctory recognition." —**J. Crosby Chapman and George Counts**, *Principles of Education*, 1924, 45

"The problem of selecting the content of the elementary school curriculum is, first, that of determining the objectives of life in terms of different needs; second, finding the means or forms of activity best adapted to meet these needs; and third, presenting these needs together with the activities for meeting them." —**George Frasier and Winfred Armentrout**, *An Introduction to Education*, 1924, 192

THE FACTORY

"In one respect the school is like a manufacturing plant. The business of a factory is to turn out a finished product with least waste of time and material, and analogously the business of the school is to turn out its product, efficient men and women, with least possible loss of time and material. This means with the least waste of the pupils' time in school and the loss of the fewest number of pupils from school until they are prepared to be helpful members of society." —**Charles McKenny**, *The Personality of the Teacher*, 1910, 107–8

THE FATAL DEFECT OF SCHOOLS

"The fatal defect of schools . . . is their unreality. The only real problem with which any school presents its pupils is the problem of getting through school. The only real interest in any textbook is an interest in getting up a subject for examination." —**C. E. Ayres**, in *New Republic*, 43:25 (May 27, 1925), re-quoted by William Kilpatrick in *Source Book in the Philosophy of Education*, 1934, 403–4

GRADE LEVEL

"Time and experience have proved the fallacy of the belief that an unselected group of thirty to forty children having begun their career in the first grade at approximately the same age might be expected to progress with equal rapidity and finish the eighth grade at the same time." —**George Strayer and N. L. Engelhardt**, *The Classroom Teacher at Work in American Schools*, 1920, 124

HAPPINESS

"Men may react against unhappiness and even draw strength from it, but happiness is the vital breath of children, the very best, if not the only, moral stimulus on which they can thrive. In all its appointments, a schoolroom for children should inspire a wholesome sense of rest and comfort, and should predispose its pupils to happiness. The teacher herself should radiate an atmosphere that is kindly, joyous and sympathetic—voice, manner and dress all conspiring to create a very paradise for childhood. One incomparable blessing bestowed on education by the kindergarten is the spirit of spontaneity and joyousness which it has introduced into the primary school" —**W. H. Payne**, *The Education of the Teacher*, 1901, 233–34

"Every child has a heaven-born right to be happy. To this end the basis of the child's gradation in the school should be the place where he can be the happiest. Shall it be with the teacher who sours everything she teaches? By no means." —**Preston Search**, *The Ideal School or, Looking Forward*, 1902, 347

"It is a paradox in educational theory that although everybody admits that the happiness of the world is an important ultimate aim, attempts to make schools minister at all directly to the happiness of scholars are often decried as undignified, 'soft pedagogy,' trifling with the serious work of education. To give them habits that will make them happy when they are forty, is allowable, even desirable, but to make them happy while they are in school is treated as a sentimental weakness." —**E. L. Thorndike**, *Education: A First Book*, 1912, 19

HIGH SCHOOL

"It is the testimony of many experienced teachers in high school . . . that pupils now come to them with less ability to master books than formerly, and with less effective habit of study." —**Emerson E. White**, *The Elements of Pedagogy*, 1886, 151

"In the high school, the 'people's college,' it was thought that society would have an institution that would respond immediately to the needs and ideals of the people. But after half or three-quarters of a century of existence the high schools...find themselves very largely college preparatory schools." —**George Herbert Betts**, *Social Principles of Education*, 1912, 256

"The origin of the term 'high school' in the American significance is not clear. The term 'higher school' in its European significance usually indicates all institutions above the elementary grade. It had been applied in a few instances to particular institutions, notably the Edinburgh High School. This Scottish institution, essentially an academy, employed the monitorial system of instruction and had achieved an international reputation. It is probable that this school gave its name to the American institution." —**Paul Monroe**, "Historic Sketch of Secondary Education," in Paul Monroe (ed.), *Principles of Secondary Education*, 1914, 61

"American educators are not in perfect agreement as to the real purpose and function of the modern high school. Should the high school be committed to the policy of general training, college preparation, or vocational efficiency? It has been generally conceded that the high school should afford pupils an opportunity to prepare for university or college. What this preparation should be has not been so well agreed upon by the representatives of the secondary schools and of the colleges." —**George Frasier and Winfield Armentrout**, *An Introduction to Education*, 1924, 206

THE JANITOR

"There is one very important factor in the care of every schoolhouse and that is the character of the work of the janitor. It is useless to talk of school hygiene and to construct sanitary buildings unless these buildings are to be cared for in the correct way. The importance of the janitor's work is often underestimated, and that person himself is all too often not given a fair chance either to know what to do or to have the tools with which to do his work as it should be done. . . . The first thing to do, in many instances, is to see that the man, woman, or boy who daily cleans the schoolroom and cares for the rest of the schoolhouse understands his problem, knows why it is harmful to do dry sweeping, appreciates the necessity for having plenty of fresh air coming into the room all the time, and realizes in a general way how important his work is." —**L. N. Hanes**, "Hygienic School Environment," in Louis Rapeer (ed.), *Educational Hygiene from the Pre-School Period to the University*, 1915, 326–27

JUNIOR HIGH SCHOOL

"A mere tinkering with seventh-and eighth-grade subjects in the old environment and with an unchanged teaching staff and supervision cannot do what we already know must be done. These internal matters of educational reorganization offer opportunities which must not be squandered. The psychological value of this junior high school is that it provides just favorable new situation for seriously conceived plans closely related to a clear educational philosophy of administration. If the junior high school is anything, it is the three-year section of our public-school system, which, with its newly developt types of 'generalized' subject-matter, 'project,' and other methods of teaching, democratic and free policy of school-management, and intimate and intensive study of the individualities of pupils, seeks to direct pupils in finding themselves by exercising their various traits, examining their various aptitudes, and making possible intelligent choice of any special sort of definite training which may be followed in the senior high school or in higher educational institutions." —**Charles Hughes Johnson**, "The Junior High School," *Proceedings of the National Education Association*, 1916, 149

"The junior high school is more a method of instruction than it is an organization. Too often we consider it as an organization rather than as a method of instruction. A junior high school is synonymous with greater opportunities for individual initiative. This is true not only from the standpoint of the pupil but from that of the teacher as well." —**Arthur Benson**, "The Present Status of the Junior High School," *Proceedings of the National Education Association*, 1920, 528

"One of the arguments advanced against the junior-high-school movement in its earlier stages was that the transfer of the seventh and eighth grades to the high school would tend to overemphasize in these grades the 'teaching of subjects' at the expense of the 'teaching of children.'" —**William Chandler Bagley and John Keith**, *An Introduction to Teaching*, 1929, 359

KINDERGARTEN

"Who ever saw anything but constant delight on the faces of the little children in a true kindergarten, where hands and heads and hearts are in continual harmonious action? The secret lies in the fact that the child's life consists of building, weaving, drawing, taking apart and putting together, and at the same time feeding the imagination for higher flights. When should this delightful play and work stop? When the primary teacher meets him at the door of a castle, fetters his active limbs to a hard seat, and imprisons his expanding mind in a narrow cell walled by unmeaning hieroglyphics? No! A thousand times no! It is cruelty to stop the blessed work done in the kindergarten." —**Francis Parker**, *Talks on Teaching*, 1883, 157

"[Kindergarten's] success is due very largely to the fact that, in general, it takes children as it finds them, and does not try to force upon them methods of thought and action suited only to the adult." —**John Mason Tyler**, *Growth and Education*, 1907, 135

"If the kindergartener [one who promotes the kindergarten] had taught the primary teacher no other lesson than that one must become a child with the children to succeed with them, she would have rendered the school an invaluable service. The teacher had stood aloof from the children, a being apparently of a different order, and occupying a different plane. The kindergartener taught her to live with the children on their own level, yet above it. The primary teacher of the present has learned the lesson, and her success is measured by her approach to the kindergarten type." —**Nina Vanderwalker**, *The Kindergarten in American Education*, 1908, 223–24

"Until the kindergarten came, the school was individualistic, not social, in its tendencies. Competition between the children rather than coöperation with them was the rule. The value of cooperative effort as a means of developing the right spirit on the part of the children toward each other has been increasingly recognized in recent years. The coöperation of the members of a class, of grade with grade, or department with department for a common end is becoming an established feature in school work. Combined effort on the part of pupils has not only made possible the decoration of schoolrooms and the beautifying of school grounds, but it has brought about a different spirit among children. Coöperative action, the principle of the kindergarten, is becoming the principle of the school." —**Nina Vandewalker**, *The Kindergarten in American Education*, 1908, 249–50

OPEN-AIR SCHOOLS

"Open-air schools are saving the lives of many children who would otherwise become the victims of tuberculosis." —**Oscar Corson**, *Our Public Schools: Their Teachers, Pupils and Patrons*, 1918, 32

"[I]n the new open-air schools, the pupils are warmed by vigorous physical exercise, so the warmth of the intellectual atmosphere of the classroom must be generated by the activity of the pupils and the teacher. The adolescent loves to work, though he hates drudgery. Fanned by a real vital interest in the work of the hour, the spirit of the class can be raised to a veritable 'glow.' The teacher who comes into the classroom 'on fire' with interest in his work and his message, not of explosive fireworks variety, but full of the zeal of a well-controlled but deep interest in his work and his students, will easily incite a similar response on the part of his class, and the intellectual warmth of the classroom will be assured." —**Herbert Foster**, *Principles of Teaching in Secondary Education*, 1921, 48

THE OVERBURDENED SCHOOL

"Thus the school came in the course of time to be regarded as the best institution for meeting those needs of the child for which other social institutions had ceased to provide. Naturally, this has led to the school's becoming overburdened with a multiplicity of tasks and duties of various kinds, many of which do not rightly belong to it. In fact, the school has willingly assumed so many of the duties that have been neglected or could not well be performed by other social institutions that it has come to be considered by many persons as a veritable dumping ground for the neglected obligations of other institutions." —**O. I. Woodley and M. Virginia Woodley**, *The Profession of Teaching*, 1917, 95

PLEASANT SCHOOLS

"A teacher who cannot make the school a pleasure to children is not a success; he is wrong or someone else is wrong. It may be the superintendent is exacting more work than can well be accomplished. It may be the texts are beyond the comprehension of the children. That some one is blundering is beyond doubt. There should be no place in an American school for a gloomy, unhappy childhood. In pleading for a happy childhood I am not pleading for an idle one. The school is a place for industry; there are things to be done; but these things can be best done in a school where a joyful eagerness spurs the children on." —**Charles McKenny**, *The Personality of the Teacher*, 1910, 27

RECESS

"What a shame it is that the modern school has no place or time for the old-fashioned free-play recess!" —**Preston Search**, *An Ideal School or, Looking Forward*, 1902, 335

"The attention of pupils is likewise to be wholesomely employed during recesses, and before and after school. Supervised play is a comparatively new element in American education, but it bids fair to eliminate a great deal of evil. The children in many country and village schools simply do not know how to play. They stand or sit around at intermissions, gossiping and staring idly at each other or at passers-by. They need to be taught lively games, organized into teams, forced really to play until they form the habit and do it spontaneously. There are several good books upon the play movement, and texts describing games and the delightful folk-dances which children love and which arouse an interest in the people of other lands." —**Frances Morehouse**, *The Discipline of the School*, 1914, 223

RESEARCH DEPARTMENTS

"Practically every large city school system now has its staff of clinical psychologists and statisticians whose business it is to devise and adapt mental and educational tests, administer them or instruct teachers in this technique, assemble and interpret the results, and suggest improvements in school organization, curriculum materials, and methods of instruction based upon their findings. Similar bureaus of research have been established in connection with some of the state departments of education, and they are sometimes attached to teachers colleges and university schools of education. Taken together, the bureaus of research constitute the most powerful single factor now working toward the improvement of education." —**William Chandler Bagley and John Keith**, *An Introduction to Teaching*, 1929, 375–76

Chapter 11
SCHOOL AS A LEARNING COMMUNITY

"[C]ommunity spirit is contagious, and boys and girls from the fourth, fifth, even sixth and seventh grades, have been known to make daily visits to the primary room 'to see what the kids are making now.' The next step is to ask if they may contribute something. Indeed, the school is running over with these opportunities for coöperation, self-help, and personal pleasure in work, but these vital, human aspects of life do not flourish in a silent, austere atmosphere. They are set going by the light of enthusiasm in the teacher's eye and by the wisdom of what seems to be undirected efforts." —**Arnold Gesell and Beatrice Gesell**, *The Normal Child and Primary Education*, 1912, 184–85

SCHOOL FAILURE

"School failure on the part of so many young adolescents certainly suggests a lack of adjustment somewhere. The school itself may be at fault in maintaining improper standards of success, or in offering to the boys and girls studies ill-suited to their real needs." —**Irving King**, *The High-School Age*, 1914, 35

SCHOOL FIRES

"Every school building should be as nearly fire-proof as possible, and the larger the building the more emphasis there should be on this factor. We have lost too many buildings and children by fire. An average of ten school buildings burn each week of the year, two each school day." —**L. W. Rapeer**, "School Sanitation Standards," in Louis Rapeer (ed.), *Educational Hygiene from the Pre-School Period to the University*, 1915, 334

SCHOOL FUNDING

"An interesting feature of school administration, fifty to seventy-five years ago, was the lottery. It came in for all sorts of uses, and some which to-day would be counted very questionable. Those referred to here, however, were legalized, had the sanction of public opinion, and were considered altogether an honorable means of raising funds. Their proceeds were in some instances considerable, and, contributed to increase the common-school fund, and the endowment of colleges; to aid in the erection of buildings, furnishing apparatus, and paying salaries.... The first steps taken (1747) toward the founding of what is now Columbia College were in the grant of a system of lotteries. Williamstown Academy, Massachusetts, was partly so founded (1790), and two years later, four lotteries were granted to the Regents of the State of New York, one eighth of whose proceeds should go to the academies, and the remainder to the common-school fund.... [The] University of Michigan and the General Board of Education were granted four lotteries, fifteen per cent of whose proceeds should be applied to the general fund. William and Mary College and Brown and Harvard Universities were recipients of like favors. Indeed, for the half-century following the Revolution there was almost no public enterprise requiring pecuniary aid that did not receive more or less State recognition and assistance through lotteries, at some time and in some section. From municipal improvements to founding and equipping colleges, establishing libraries, initiating and augmenting school-funds, and building churches, the lottery was a common source of relief. One writer, speaking for Rhode Island alone, says lotteries were made 'to contribute to churches in Providence, Newport, Bristol, and half a dozen other towns; by Baptist, Methodist, Presbyterian, and Congregational faith.' They were the church fairs of our grandfathers—a device whose function, as a source of general revenue, possesses a decided historic interest." —**Richard Boone**, *Education in the United States*, 1893, 87–88

"Roughly, one and a half per cent. of the total property of our country is held by the public, or in practical trust for the public, for service as school grounds, buildings, equipment and endowment. This may seem a very small fraction, and all truly patriotic men and women will certainly work to increase it, but it is beyond anything that the world has hitherto known. It seems pitifully small when one learns that in three years' time the nation expends as much for alcoholic beverages,– or that the cost of the Civil War in pensions alone would have paid for it twice over,–or that, by cutting the expense of our army and navy to what it was in 1897, we could double school facilities and endowment in ten years." —**E. L. Thorndike**, *Education: A First Book*, 1912, 276

"The American public school...depends chiefly upon local support for its maintenance and it progress. This means that there will be striking inequalities among the schools not only throughout the country but within each state. Writing in 1922, George Strayer made the following contrasts: 'The states vary greatly in their ability to support education. From the latest available data the true wealth *per capita* is found to vary in the several states from $726 to $5038. The contrast is quite as startling if the true wealth per pupil enrolled in schools is taken. Here the variation runs from $2561 to $19,377.'"
—**William Chandler Bagley and John Keith**, *An Introduction to Teaching*, 1929, 302–3

SCHOOL REFORM

"Every period doubtless seems to those who live and work in it to be more fruitful of reform than any preceding time in the world's history. Perhaps we exaggerate the extent and importance of the school reforms of the last twenty years, but they seem to be broad in scope and profound in meaning for the future." —**Charles Judd**, *Evolution of a Democratic School System*, 1918, 71

SCHOOL SIZE

"A high school of a hundred scholars is vastly better than our present gigantic establishments, with their two or three thousand young people gathered from the four quarters of the town, and forced to spend two, or even three, hours a day in the nervous and altogether uncompensated act of transit." — **C. Hanford Henderson**, *Education and the Larger Life*, 1902, 217

THE SCHOOL WAGON DRIVER

"[T]he ability properly to drive a team and to look after the physical safety of the children are not the only qualifications drivers must possess. If such were the case it would be far less difficult to secure first-class drivers than it is. The question of moral influence plays one of the most important parts in the transporting of school children. The man who conveys pupils to and from school should be as clean and wholesome as the teacher who instructs them during school hours. Children are imitators always, and will be influenced by their driver as quickly and naturally as by their teacher. It is universally agreed that no man who uses intoxicating liquors should be employed as a driver. It should likewise be agreed that no man whose habits or standards are unworthy of imitation should be numbered among those who transport pupils to and from schools." —**George Betts and Otis Hall**, *Better Rural Schools*, 1914, 317–18

SINGLE SEX CLASSROOMS

"There is some denial of the statement that in early adolescence boys and girls advance more satisfactorily if segregated in certain subjects; but on the whole the evidence tends to prove it. More and better experimentation is needed before a conclusion can be confidently accepted." —**Thomas Briggs**, *The Junior High School*, 1920, 17

"A study of adolescence shows that from twelve to sixteen, at least, girls and boys differ in tastes, development and degrees of maturity. 'The girl at the same age is older than the boy,' and most boys appear at a disadvantage when placed in classes with girls of the same age. Authorities also agree that, during early adolescence at least, the ends of discipline are better served where the sexes are kept apart and the boys are taught by men and the girls by women. Notwithstanding the many advantages of our co-educational system, the foremost students of education in the United States are looking with favor upon the separation of the boys and girls for at least a part of the time and for the purpose of providing different lines of work during a part of the period covered by the grammar grades and the high school." —**William Chandler Bagley**, "Adolescence," *Public School Methods* 6 (1921): 301–2

STUDENT DESKS

"Dewey, trying to find some school desks suitable for work, thus narrates his experience: 'Some years ago I was looking about the school-supply stores in the city, trying to find desks and chairs which seemed thoroughly suitable from all points of view—artistic, hygienic, and educational. We had a good deal of difficulty in finding what we needed, and one dealer, more intelligent than the rest, made this remark, "I am afraid we have not what you want. You want something at which the children may work; these are all for listening." That tells the story of the traditional education.'" —**Charles DeGarmo**, *Principles of Secondary Education*, 1907, 167

"According to an advertisement in the *American School Board Journal*, 95 per cent of the desks made and sold are of the stationary type." —**Ned Dearborn**, *An Introduction to Teaching*, 1925, 150

UNHEALTHY CLASSROOMS

"When we reflect that, according to Hesse, 35,000 bacteria have been found in every cubic metre of air of a school room at the end of the session; and, according to Ignatieff, that a pupil would thus in a five hours' session inhale 44,655 germs; and that Erismann has found many kinds of micro-organisms and moulds in the school room; and that the death of certain animals has been produced by injection of liquids saturated with condensed vapours carrying the toxic products of the school room—it seems rational that we should adopt, for the preservation of the health of the children, the same measures deemed necessary in our better hospitals. Accumulations of carbonic-acid gas are certainly to be avoided; but even these are not nearly so dangerous to certain susceptible children as other toxic products not so easily detected." — **Preston Search**, *An Ideal School or, Looking Forward*, 1902, 87

WHEN A STUDENT LEAVES SCHOOL

"When the pupil leaves school he should be prepared to launch out and pursue his own aims with success." —**Charles McMurry**, *The Elements of General Method*, 1895, 211

THE WORK FORCE

"The National Education Association, in its 1909 report, publishes the startling figures that fifty per cent of our skilled mechanics are foreign-born and trained and that ninety-eight per cent of the foremen in New York manufactories were educated across the water. In other words, Americans to fill such positions are not to found." —**Ruth Mary Weeks**, *The People's School: A Study in Vocational Training*, 1912, 20

Chapter Twelve

Students

Until the 1930s, children in school were called pupils, not students. S. E. Davis (*The Teacher's Relationships*, 1930, 187) said that "pupils" were school children who were taught, while "students" were self-directed learners such as those found at the college level. However, Davis reported that the word "students" was beginning to appear in the literature in reference to elementary school children. He was not certain that it was appropriate to use the word "students" for pupils below college age.

There were comments about students who were self-indulgent and students who dropped out of school. There was concern about the effects of poverty and Thorndike warned about making unwarranted generalizations about racial differences among students.

DROP OUTS

"The records of high schools show that a very large proportion, sometimes as high as fifty per cent of the pupils who enter them, drop out at the end of the first year. And a further study will reveal the fact that at least eight out of ten of the pupils that have thus dropped out have 'failed to pass' in Latin or algebra, or both." —**William Hawley Smith**, *All the Children of All the People*, 1912, 193–94

"At the end of two years of the high-school course, sixty-eight per cent of the boys and sixty-one per cent of the girls 'who were certain as to their probable future occupation had dropped out' of school, while sixty percent of the boys and fifty-five per cent of the girls, irrespective of whether they had a future occupation in mind or not, had left school at the same time. 'This would show that the boy or girl, especially the boy, who has some definite occupation in mind lasts a trifle better than the boy with no such determination.'" —**Irving King**, *The High-School Age*, 1914, 161

"[M]any pupils have dropped out of school or failed to work with enthusiasm because the subjects offered to them were artificial and unsuited to their needs." —**Charles Judd**, *The Evolution of a Democratic School* System, 1918, 101–2

"Three-fourths who enter school reach the sixth grade of school.

"One-half who enter school complete elementary school.

"One-third who enter school enter high school.

"One-eighth who enter school complete high school." —**George Frasier and Winfred Armentrout**, *An Introduction to Education*, 1924, 197

THE ME GENERATION

Dislike is a shameful excuse for failing to do one's assigned duty. Good soldiers are faithful, obedient, dependable, in every kind of weather, under all circumstances. Much, very much, of sound old-fashioned Puritan devotion to duty we need to preach, suggest, practice, and illustrate, if our schools and our nation are to fulfill their trust. The age is one of self-indulgence, and a deplorably soft pedagogy has exalted personal liking over sensible requirement." —**Frances Morehouse**, *The Discipline of the School*, 1914, 231

POVERTY

"Therefore, you educators of the people, look to places where your pupils live; look into the halls and rooms which they call their home; learn the need and misery with which their parents must contend and, if you do so, you will meet your pupils with understanding eyes and warmer hearts. You cannot drive this misery out of the world, but you learn charity when you perceive what shadows that misery casts upon the school." —**Hermann Weimer**, *The Way to the Heart of the Pupil*, 1913, 168

RACIAL DIFFERENCES

"Far too little is known of original racial differences in intellectual and moral capacities, and the errors of educational practice have here commonly been to exaggerate differences that do exist and to imagine many that do not." — **E. L. Thorndike**, *Education: A First Book*, 1912, 68

RESPECT FOR SOCIAL AND ETHICAL LAW

"A deep-seated respect for social and ethical law is needed in our country. The sooner children learn that they have social and moral obligations which are bound to be respected, the better it is for them. Girls and boys have a certain amount of energy which is bound to get an outlet somehow; if early led to love nature, they will become its protectors. Such children will not vandalize nature; when grown up they are sure to become good, law-abiding members of society. This makes for a morally sound citizenship." —**Joseph K. Hart**, *Educational Resources of Village and Rural Communities*, 1914, 222

Chapter Thirteen

Subject Matter

Much of the change that occurred in democratic schools concerned subject matter. Teachers worked to organize and present subject matter in ways that enabled all children to learn. No longer was subject matter to be taught as an intellectual exercise without application to the lives of students; the new education was to be personalized and paced to the needs and abilities of the students. While individualizing was the goal, teachers were often reminded that it was children who were being taught, not subject matter.

Bobbitt spoke of students who were able to master complex mathematic concepts but could not think quantitatively in other subjects. Parker wrote of the dangers of teaching geography to students who never ventured from the classroom. And, as early as the 1880s, educators called for an end to the teaching of grammar; they argued there was no relationship between memorizing the rules of language and the effective use of language.

Other changes called for a rethinking of how subjects were taught. Joseph Mayer Rice, often referred to as "the father of educational research," presented data to demonstrate that the effective teaching of spelling should consume no more that fifteen minutes a day. To teach spelling beyond fifteen minutes did not yield additional achievement.

There was debate (as there is today) over the use of phonics versus thinking or whole language as the proper way to teach reading. Physical education was introduced as an important school subject. The drafting of men into the armed forces during the recently ended World War I revealed that "thirty-four per cent of the men between twenty-one and thirty-one years of age were found unfit for general military service." The blame for the poor physical condition of the population was placed on the schools. Life skills such as sex education, drug education, and temperance became school subjects.

ARITHMETIC

"Arithmetic is an essential factor in every step of human progress; still, the subject as a school study has been held until to-day almost entirely apart from anything like practical education. That which is most deeply rooted in tradition has a sort of benumbing effect upon the intellect; the profound reverence of the average scholar for the past making him accept the logic of his ancestors without question." —**Francis Parker**, *Talks on Pedagogics*, 1894, 64

COMPOSITION

"Children are inclined to think that composing is entirely different from talking, and far more difficult. This notion often causes them to dread composition, and to be unnatural in their attempts to compose. It is therefore quite important to correct all such notions. The pupils must be made to see first of all that it is possible to *write* thoughts as well as to *talk* thoughts, and that writing and talking are somewhat equivalent as modes of expressing thoughts. This point cleared up, it becomes evident to pupils that composing is not an attempt to say what they do not know or cannot think, but just the opposite. The relation of talking and writing is best taught by requiring pupils to talk their thoughts before writing them, and to write them just as they would talk them." —**Charles C. Boyer**, *Principles and Methods of Teaching*, 1902, 182

DRUG EDUCATION

"Every one of the 48 States, the District of Columbia, and the Territories of the United States provide for instruction in the evil effects of narcotics, except that Arkansas merely provides for instruction in human physiology and hygiene which might logically include narcotic drug addiction." . . . "Thirty-eight jurisdictions provide for compulsory 'habit forming drug' education in all of the schools maintained in part or wholly by State funds; 11 make specific provision for such education in public elementary schools, 1 in the public high schools, 6 in the public normal schools, and 3 in the public military and naval academies or public colleges and universities. Of course it must be remembered that the term 'public school,' which is used in 32 State laws, would by interpretation include the public elementary, junior high, senior high, and normal schools, also public colleges and universities, if any." —**E. George Payne**, "Narcotic Addiction as an Educational Problem," in **E. George Payne**, *Readings in Educational Sociology*, 1934, 122–23

GEOGRAPHY

"Long experience has taught teachers that the child who learns the text of a Primary Geography rarely ever dreams that the objects about which he reads are ever before his eyes when in the open air. The teacher thinks how much better it is for him to learn the definition, made by some great educator (!)—in other words, some job book-maker,–than it is to see the reality in all its beauty and power. The German teachers learned long ago that the only way to teach Geography is by observation in field excursions. Yet with us the fetich of word-learning holds thousands of teachers soul-bound by its superstitions. They still believe that the words are of more educational value than the things themselves!" —**Francis Parker**, *Talks on Pedagogics*, 1894, 163

GRAMMAR

"Through the erroneous notion that English grammar teaches how to speak and write the English language correctly, textbooks in grammar are put into the hands of young children, and their minds are crammed with definitions and rules concerning the philosophic structure of language, and this before their mental powers are so far developed as to comprehend the principles which are sought to be given. The matter memorized, having failed to reach the understanding, becomes a hindrance rather than a help to education." — **James Johonnot**, *Principles and Practice of Teaching*, 1881, 57

"The old-time attempt to teach the art of using good English, by means of technical grammar, is an illustration of . . . error. This attempt was based on the false notion that skill in speech and writing is a necessary result of knowledge of the rules of language—an error still too common in American schools." —**Emerson E. White**, *The Elements of Pedagogy*, 1886, 128

"Many good people, teachers and others, say that the language of children is suffering because grammar is not thoroughly taught now. As a matter of fact the language of children is much better than when grammar was more persistently taught. The gain is not sufficient to occasion hysterics of joy among us teachers, but it is a gain." —**B. C. Gregory**, *Better Schools*, 1912, 204

"A generation ago technical grammar, the rules and principles of the English language, was commonly taught in the fourth and fifth grades (e.g., the eight parts of speech), but now we try to arouse children to a keen and practical interest in stories, in excursions, and in lively topics in nature study for composition." —**Charles McMurry**, *Teaching by Projects: A Basis for Purposeful Study*, 1927, 67

LANGUAGE

"The teacher's effort in language and composition work should be to preserve the spontaneous, free self-expression, characteristic of most children upon entering school, and to secure in them steady growth in the mastery of style and form, so that both their oral and written expression may be effective. When playing, children talk naturally and freely about their experiences. They express themselves forcibly and with delightful spontaneity, although with many crudities. The school should seek to encourage and develop this oral self-expression. Written expression should be introduced gradually from grade to grade. As the children acquire the ability, it should increase in prominence. If the school can bring the children's speech and writing up to accepted standards without crushing spontaneity and freedom in expression, the ends sought through language teaching will be accomplished." —**H. B Wilson and G. M. Wilson**, *The Motivation of School Work*, 1921, 71

LITERATURE

"What is the fundamental purpose in the teaching of literature? The most frequent rely is, The *appreciation of literature*. Almost never do they say that it is an understanding and appreciation of human-kind and human affairs and the general setting of the great human drama." —**Franklin Bobbitt**, *The Curriculum*, 1918, 238

MATHEMATICS

"Teaching children numerical figures without their application is merely cultivating the recollection of meaningless forms, without any exercise of the judgment. There is not the slightest exercise of the judgment in simply repeating the fact that four and five are nine. A judgment is the essential element of reason, and when a child is actually measuring objects he is reasoning. When he is learning the figures in the multiplication table he is cultivating his verbal memory, to be sure, but working even in this at a disadvantage because ignoring the laws of necessity, of use, and association, reasoning having nothing whatever to do with the process." —**Francis Parker**, *Talks on Pedagogics*, 1894, 78–79

"*When would you teach the child his multiplication table?* I do not know that I would teach it to him at all; I would probably let him learn it. And yet it is highly important the child should have careful drill in the alphabets of numbers during this period. Instead of making him commit meaningless tables of numbers, I would place the common tables in large characters on great charts on the walls so that the child could get his table help at any time by an immediate glance at the table form. An abundance of calculations soon makes the child familiar with the fundamental products; and after a time he will himself shortcut the process by mastering the missing links." —**Preston Search**, *An Ideal School or, Looking Forward*, 1902, 133

"The major criticism of the mathematical teaching in the general education of present-day high school and college is its colossal failure to develop habits of quantitative-mindedness on the part of the population. Those who have climbed the steeps of our usual algebra, geometry, and trigonometry, appear to think about as vaguely and loosely in the fields of civics, economics, and the like as those who have not. The system has been given a long fair trial. The results are disappointing." —**Franklin Bobbitt**, *How to Make a Curriculum*, 1924, 150

PHONICS VS. WHOLE LANGUAGE

"When pupils have by practice associated the sounds or phonic powers of letters with their forms, they might be wisely taught 'to make out' new words by synthesizing the phonic elements which compose them. This is the synthetic method of teaching words. Pupils may also be taught to divide certain printed words into syllables, and then to synthesize these syllabic elements into the spoken words." —**Emerson E. White**, *The Elements of Pedagogy*, 1886, 170

"The 'Phonetic Method' [used to teaching reading] that was advocated some years ago, is impracticable, because it requires the pupil to know about fourteen new letters in addition to our twenty-six, in order to avoid the diacritical contrivances. The transition to twenty-six letters and the diacritical marks is necessary after all, and is complicated rather than promoted by the introductory phonetic system. If, however, the English language were absolutely phonetic, this system would have some real merit. It is not likely that the method will ever be revived." —**Charles C. Boyer**, *Principles and Methods of Teaching*, 1902, 122

"A pupil should never grow into the way of thinking that 'sounding words' for himself is in itself a virtue. The virtue lies in finding out *what the book says.* The more readily he can do this, the better. The use of phonics is 'the only way out' if the eye fails to recognize the words that stand in the way." —**Thomas Briggs and Lotus Coffman**, *Reading in Public Schools*, 1911, 91

"The place of phonics in teaching primary reading continues to be a debated question. Many specialists in the field of reading refuse to take a stand on whether to teach phonics or not to teach phonics. Apparently no hard-and-fast rule can be laid down. Slow children are sometimes benefited by the use of phonics; at the same time there are other children who are handicapped by such instruction. It is likely, therefore, that the teaching of phonics should be incidental, or limited to those pupils who appear to need such instruction." —**Walter Monroe and Ruth Streitz**, *Directing Learning in the Elementary School*, 1932, 167

PHYSICAL EDUCATION

"In the first national army draft in 1917, when the physical standards were kept high, thirty-four per cent of the men between twenty-one and thirty-one years of age were found unfit for general military service. This is an indictment directly of the society in which these men had grown to maturity, and indirectly of the health service which has been offered in our public school system. It has been discovered that physical education and health service can be administered most economically and most efficiently in connection with the public schools." —**George Strayer and N. L. Engelhardt**, *The Classroom Teacher at Work in American Schools*, 1920, 17

"If the physical activities developed in school for health purposes are not made highly enjoyable their chance for persistence after one leaves school is very small. . . . [F]or those whose work provides enough physical exercise for normal health, some additional participation in games or sports highly enjoyed is probably of value in giving wholesome tone and attitude to body and mind. The mortality among business and professional men of middle age seemingly due to their sedentary habits is so large that it constitutes a very great social loss. The school should provide the knowledge of health conduct necessary throughout life." —**Frederick Bonser**, *The Elementary School Curriculum*, 1922, 47–48

READING

"A well-known college professor, in response to a school superintendent's question as to what would better the preparation of students for college, replied: 'Teach them how to read.'" —**S. H. Clark**, *How to Teach Reading in the Public School*, 1898, 11

"These words will bear repeating: The chief function of reading in the school is to create a habit of thought-getting, to make every pupil feel that he does not want to abandon a lesson in reading, or his reading of other lessons, until he has mastered the thought that is in them. If a teacher can accomplish this and at the same time put in the way of her pupils the right methods of thought-getting, she has accomplished the greatest thing in intellectual education." —**Charles McMurry**, ed., *Public School Methods, Vol. 3*, 1912, 136

"The child must learn to read before he can read to learn." —**Charles McMurry**, ed., *Public School Methods, Vol. 3*, 1912, 154

SCIENCE

"The methods of teaching science should be in harmony with its aims, and this means that methods employed in teaching other subjects will not be satisfactory. There should be no formal drill; instead, the pupils should derive their facts from the study of real materials. If books are used, it should be after the examination of the actual materials in the form of leaves, flowers, roots, trees, soil, insects, birds, and so forth. Isolated facts will be of little use, but an attempt should be made to discover characteristics by which one species, family, and class may be distinguished from another. This will mean giving special attention to likenesses and differences." —**John Almack and Albert Lang**, *The Beginning Teacher*, 1928, 373

SEX EDUCATION

"Considerable agitation has arisen over the suggestion that sex education be imparted to the young. The fundamental opposition from a failure to recognize that sex education is constantly being acquired by children. Furthermore, there has been a possible lack of understanding that the real problem does not consist in determining whether sex education should be given to all children, but under what conditions and by which teachers. Ignorance and innocence in childhood, in so far as sex themes are concerned, are not one and the same thing. There may be chastity with a full knowledge and understanding of the facts of life, or there may be gross immorality without any true knowledge of the underlying physiology or hygiene of sex life." —**Ira S. Wile**, "Sex Hygiene and Sex Education," in Louis Rapeer (ed.), *Educational Hygiene from the Pre-School Period to the University*, 1915, 549

"[T]he sphere where the child receives the least light; that realm where the light he does receive is distorted so that he is all confused as to meanings and values; that realm which, experience shows, is the source from which springs most of the cases of mental disturbance—the realm of sex. We noted above that every child is taught that hunger is proper but that to gratify hunger he must go through preliminary steps—*work, money, buy,* and *eat.* Why cannot he be taught that sexual appetite is proper but that to gratify it he must go through certain steps—*sex hunger* (libido), *courtship, marriage,* and *gratification?* But he is not so taught. Teachers and parents teach him nothing; they exhibit the greatest horror if the child expresses a desire to learn. If they teach him anything it is likely to be that the whole subject is indecent, including any impulses of this nature that he may have. He learns secretly. Thus the very knowledge itself is an immoral thing to him. He gains the knowledge and is then ashamed that he knows. There are persons who in later years never lose the idea that the whole subject of sex is vile." —**John J. B. Morgan**, *The Psychology of the Unadjusted School Child*, 1930, 80–81

SPELLING

"I beg to offer the suggestion that not more than fifteen minutes daily be devoted to spelling, including both study and recitation. As I have shown elsewhere, additional time given to this subject is not rewarded by additional return." —**Joseph Mayer Rice**, *The Rational Spelling Book: Part One*, 1898, 6

"Pupils will often use words before they meet them in a spelling book, and some of them they will misspell. Again, after they have studied a word they may misspell it in their written exercises. There appears to be no way to meet these difficulties except for each pupil to have an individual list of his own 'demons' or 'stumbling blocks' which he is conquering by special study." —**Daniel Starch and George A. Mirick**, *The Test and Study Speller*, 1921, x

SUBJECT MATTER

"So far as subject matter is concerned knowledge is either employed to generate power, somewhat as dumb-bells are used to strengthen the muscles, or it quietly passes into structure by a process of absorption and assimilation, or it is simply held in the mind as useful furniture ready on occasion to be turned to practical account." —**W. H. Payne**, *The Education of Teachers*, 1901, 190

"For practical consideration we may classify subject matter into four groups: (1) that which is essential, (2) that which is useful, (3) that which is desirable, and (4) that which is undesirable." —**Ned Dearborn**, *An Introduction to Teaching*, 1925, 150

TEMPERANCE

"The W.C.T.U [Women's Christian Temperance Union] is responsible for the introduction of temperance instruction in the public schools, and great credit is due the organization for its efforts in this direction. But not all teachers have been in full sympathy with the movement, and, while fulfilling the letter of the law, have not entered into the spirit of the opportunity offered. Sources of information, both scientific and statistical, have not always been reliable, methods of teaching have not always been approvable, and in contemplation of these facts, I am almost forced to say that a great deal of this half-hearted, purposeless and incompetent instruction might better have been omitted." —**Randall Saunders**, *The Teacher and the Times*, 1911, 83

TYPEWRITERS

"That the question of typewriting vs. pen writing has a strong bearing on the matter of health can be readily recognized by observing the erect posture assumed by the manipulator of the machine and the cramped-chested position of the average penman. Doubtless, children brought up to the habitual use of the typewriter would show an increased lung capacity over those who have spent hours every day bending over their desks in the execution of pen writing. It is the constant talk that our modern school system overstrains the nervous system of the child, and all sorts of methods are proposed for relieving this strain. Probably no better thing can be suggested for lessening the constant strain necessary in the use of the pen than the substitution for it of the typewriter, where the hand movement becomes mechanical. One writer who spoke of the 'nerve-destroying pen,' made a shot which went straight to the mark when he coined that phrase." —**Frank Waldo**, "The Educational Use of the Typewriter," *Education*, XXII (April 1902): 486

Chapter Fourteen

Teacher Preparation and Development

As public schools changed so did the call for the preparation of teachers. Colleges and universities began to develop teacher education programs, but in some places the old methods of teacher training persisted. Normal schools with summer institutes remained a major means to prepare teachers, and as late as 1920 there were still school districts that hired high school graduates to teach in the elementary schools. This meant that in rural areas, sixteen-, seventeen-, and eighteen-year-old girls with only a high school education were teaching elementary school children. There was then, as now, a severe shortage of a well-prepared teacher corps.

Teacher education programs and certification were criticized for allowing easy access to the profession. Many who were unqualified and individuals of low intellectual ability were able to receive teaching credentials. Because there was a shortage of teachers it was possible to become a teacher without any professional training at all.

In 1903 Neet bemoaned the practice of hiring individuals who learned to become teachers with only on the job training, similar to the current practice of placing uncertified teachers in the classroom today.

Teacher meetings were not highly valued and Davis wondered if there would be any attendance if they were not compulsory. Mentoring was a recommended strategy for helping new teachers.

EASY ENTRY INTO THE PROFESSION

"Thousands of schools are yet taught by those who have had little or no schooling in advance of that given in the rural schools themselves. In a middle western state one girl who failed in the examinations for passing from the eighth grade into the high school of her home town, took the teachers' examination, obtained a certificate and became a teacher in the rural schools!" —**George Betts and Otis Hall**, *Better Rural Schools*, 1914, 132

"For the most part, the only selection provided [to become a teacher] is that which occurs automatically as individuals without guidance pass through the educational system. The barriers which guard the occupation at the lower levels are formidable only to the mentally defective or the criminally minded.Students who do not reach the low standard of intellectual attainment required by those who employ teachers are of course excluded from the profession. Likewise those of doubtful moral character are eliminated. But, as a general rule, young men and women who offer themselves for teaching if they are able to meet certain formal requirements which make very limited demands on either capacity or training are gladly accepted." —**J. Crosby Chapman and George Counts**, *Principles of Education*, 1924, 581

EDUCATIONAL LEADERSHIP

"[T]raining schools for teachers do not perform their full duty in accepting and conforming to present educational standards, but that educational leadership is an indispensable part of their office. The thing needful is improvement of education, not simply by turning out teachers who can do better the things that are now necessary to do, but rather by changing the conception of what constitutes education." —**John Dewey**, "The Relation of Theory to Practice in Education," *The Third Yearbook of the National Society for the Scientific Study of Education*, Part I, 1904, 30

IN-SERVICE EDUCATION

"A growing teacher insures successful teaching. Opportunities for professional development are offered through reading courses, extension courses, correspondence courses, summer session study, travel, experimental or laboratory work, and individual reading. Bagley characterizes these various forms as 'in-service' education." —**Ned Dearborn**, *An Introduction to Teaching*, 1925, 21

MENTORS

"Because of lacking experience, the young teacher makes many mistakes which, to the highly sensitive professional conscience, may seem to be nothing less than terrible, the unforgivable pedagogic sin. It is here that a sympathetic older teacher can shorten the period of useless mourning and chagrin by helpful counsel. Later, surveyed in retrospect, the unhappy experience may be viewed calmly as an inevitable part of living and learning; and the sooner the lesson of the error is capitalized for future guidance, the better."
—**S. E. Davis**, *The Teacher's Relationships*, 1930, 259

TEACHER SHORTAGE

"There will be no adequate appreciation of our present and future predicament until the public comes to realize that a shortage of teachers means a shortage of *well-trained and highly competent teachers*. It is easy enough, especially with present salary schedules, to get inexperienced, untrained, and poor teachers. A real problem arises when an attempt is made to get a liberal supply of well-trained and highly competent teachers despite the failure of the public to appreciate and support such efforts." —**Ervin E. Lewis**. *Personnel Problems of the Teaching Staff*, 1925, 32–33

TEACHER TRAINING

"To present the teacher with the actual situation he will meet upon entering the service of the public schools, we shall need to have him observe the typical schoolroom, which will be something like the following: A group of about forty children is divided into two classes taught by one teacher, usually a woman; the physical features, seating, lighting, heating, and ventilation, are passable; considerable blackboard space is available, and illustrative material, maps, globes, charts, etc., is provided; while one class recites, the other prepares the lesson to be recited immediately; sometimes, between recitation periods, the teacher spends a few moments answering desultory questions. This, in brief, is the general type of situation in which our prospective teacher will be placed." —**C. R. Maxwell**, *The Observation of Teaching*, 1917, 19–20

"Teacher training schools teach young men and women how to begin teaching and inspire them to keep on learning how to solve school problems all up the line. The mission of a teacher training institution is to teach students how to learn how to teach after they begin to teach. Teaching is a new art every year with every teacher." —**A. E. Winship**, *Danger Signals for Teachers*, 1919, 58

TEACHERS' MEETINGS

Teachers' meetings should "be organized with the definite idea of involving the cooperation and contribution of teachers, and that it be not in a place where teachers go to receive instructions which might better be handed to them on a mimeographed sheet." —**George Strayer and N. L. Engelhardt**, *The Classroom Teacher at Work in American Schools*, 1920, 55

Teachers' meetings "should be thoroughly planned and administered. The meeting must not degenerate into pointless, boresome discussion, or into a desultory talk-fest. Neither the speaker on the platform nor a member of the audience has the right to make long digressions or to raise irrelevant questions. This fault is one very commonly complained of by teachers. There should be a time limit on the meeting, the discussion should be kept moving, and a summary made." —**A. S. Barr and William Burton**, *The Supervision of Instruction*, 1926, 413

"Some teachers seem to regard teachers' meetings as a necessary nuisance, and others even discount their necessity. Unless compelled by regulation or administrative necessity, one would be led to believe that there would seldom be a quorum if he took seriously the sideline comments of teachers." —**S. E. Davis**, *The Teacher's Relationships*, 1930, 111

TRAINED VS. UNTRAINED TEACHERS

"So a teacher to become skillful must have practice in the art of teaching. This practice may be obtained in two ways:

"1. A student may obtain it by teaching as a student-teacher under the direction of a skillful training-teacher in a training school.

"2. A teacher may obtain it by teaching in his own school without having any practice before, and thus acquire the skill by experience without the direction of a training-teacher.

"It is evident that learning to teach in the latter way is pretty hard on the pupils upon which the teacher practices. It is too much a matter of experiment, and is very much like a physician's learning to practice medicine by experimenting upon his patients. But everywhere almost the children in our schools are victims of such experimenting…. It is a deplorable set of conditions which compels persons to teach who have merely enough education in the subjects to secure licenses, and it is certainly not a less deplorable set of conditions which compels teachers to experiment thus with the innocent lives of our children." —**George Neet**, *Studies in Pedagogy*, 1903, 168–69

"The untrained teacher's interest is likely to be exclusively in the subject-matter he is teaching—his specialty; the trained teacher's interest in his subject is also great, but his interest in his pupil is equally great, and furnishes the guide to the sequence and correlation of topics and to the distribution of emphasis in instruction. In other words, the untrained teacher is concerned about having his pupils learn as much of the subject as possible; the trained teacher also wishes his pupils to learn the subject, but he teaches the pupils by means of the subject—the subject is a means to an end, not merely an end in itself." —**Paul Hanus**, *A Modern School*, 1905, 272–73

"The normal schools were founded to meet the need of properly equipping class-room teachers for the elementary schools, and this need they have never outgrown and never can; it is fundamental imperative, perennial. They have shed their beneficent influence over thousands of class-rooms, and, by making clear the great distinction between a trained and an untrained teacher, both at the outset and throughout the teacher's entire career, they have, almost single-handed, gradually transformed the calling of the elementary teacher from a mere routine into a profession." —**Paul Hanus**, *A Modern School*, 1905, 225

THE VALUE OF EDUCATIONAL BOOKS

"Even teachers of experience will agree that often, when they read educational books without a specific purpose in view, not much of the material remains long in the mind in a form definite enough to influence their teaching. On the other hand, when a teacher consults a book in order to obtain help in the solution of a teaching problem, and, having found what he wants, immediately puts it to use, he is more likely to remember what he has learned and to use it again." —**William Stark**, *Every Teacher's Problems*, 1922, 355

Chapter Fifteen

Teachers and Teaching

A great deal was said about teachers. Some writers expressed great admiration for the dedication and hard work of teachers. There was discussion of whether good teachers were "born" or if they became effective through proper development. It appears that many teachers spent their entire existence involved with schoolwork and students to the extend they had no life away from work. There was concern about the stress of teaching and if the stress was related to frequent teacher turnover.

Bagley reported that half of elementary teachers left teaching by the end of the fourth year of teaching—this rate of turnover is still with us today. There are also descriptions of the reasons why teachers were not rehired by their school districts; again, many of these reason could apply to teachers today.

There were metaphors to describe the role of teacher—the general and the mediator. Writers wrote about good teachers and the qualities that made them good. Good teachers teach children, not subjects, they have vision; they are reflective, patient, and persistent. Most effective teachers are in control of themselves and their classrooms because they can separate emotion from good practice.

Technology enters the picture under this heading. Thomas Edison proclaimed the motion picture as the best teacher; he argued that the movies could hold student interest better than any human teacher. Advocates of radio education proposed that radio broadcasts could become the "free, common school" for all citizens.

BEGINNING TEACHERS

"Two things are important in the beginner: first, close watchfulness for her own mistakes; second, a willingness to receive criticism and advice from those wiser than herself. Above all, remember that if the first day did not go entirely as you hoped, there is tomorrow in which to improve upon today." —**Florence Milner**, *The Teacher*, 1912, 31

"The beginning teacher usually undergoes a period of despair in attempting to find specific causes for a general dissatisfaction. Teachers in this confused state of mind, whether experienced or inexperienced, are best helped by the advice of a skillful and sympathetic supervisor." —**Douglas Waples**, *Problems in Classroom Method*, 1929, 44

BORN TEACHERS

"Some people will never get tired of telling us that 'teachers are born, not made,' and not altogether without reason, for some innate qualities are essential for the making of, at any rate, the best teachers. That *all* teachers are not 'born' is obvious. The main trouble is that the 'born' teachers are not born fast enough to supply the ever increasing demand. This leaves us the alternative either to 'make' teachers or to get along with 'makeshift' teachers. We do both. Hundreds of permanent training schools throughout the country are at work 'to make' teachers and aid 'born' teachers. Unfortunately, however, many so-called teachers of the present day can neither be said to have been 'born' or to have been 'made.' They are neither natural teachers nor professionally trained teachers—they are mere makeshifts, who neither pursue their work for the love of it nor because they are especially equipped, but simply because they must do something." —**Harold Foght**, *The American Rural School*, 1912, 70–71

"We say that some persons are 'born' teachers; but this only means that they more clearly and easily seize the fundamental principles underlying instruction, and more skilfully put them into practise. But even 'born' teachers need to be trained in the principles of their art. For such training will save them from many mistakes; and a teacher's mistakes are always made at the expense of some child's growth and development. His acquisition of skill as a teacher has cost his pupils dear." —**George Betts and Otis Hall**, *Better Rural Schools*, 1914, 141

DEMAND FOR GOOD TEACHERS

"The demand for good teachers was never so great as now, and no matter where you are if your work is good it will attract attention." —**Francis Parker**, *Talks on Teaching*, 1883, 16

DISTANCE EDUCATION

"In a word, it is possible and probable that radio broadcasting will become a great free common school in the not distant future—a common school with classes numbering thousands; following the best methods and employing the most competent instructors; attended by older pupils who will feel no embarrassment by reason of advanced years, and by younger who will be in no danger of chafing at rules and restrictions. In addition to the usual grade and high-school courses, special instruction can be arranged for boys who are being trained in specific trades and for men who are engaged in them, so as to improve their vocational ability and increase their general information. Every radio school can be expanded into a university center. Lecture courses can be planned in the fine arts, biology, literature, and the physical sciences. 'Guest' professors—great specialists and savants—will be glad to appear on this platform and deliver their messages in a hall that has no limiting walls; statesmen will expound their theories of polity, and famous writers and artists will grace the curriculum with the fine touch of their vision." —**Martin Rice**, "The Future of Radio Education," *The Journal of the National Education Association* (March 1924): 82

THE EARLY SCHOOLMASTER

"The earlier school-teachers were nearly all men, and they taught the community in which they worked, as well as the children. The teacher was commonly a student thoughtful, judicious in his conduct, and devoted to his work. He may not have really known very much, judged by our present-day standards, but to the community he seemed very learned. The pupils who came to him were of all ages, from four or five to twenty or twenty-one. Grading, state or county courses of study, and uniform textbooks had not yet been introduced. Each pupil studied about what he chose, and from the book he happened to have. Reading and recitations were individual; sums were worked on the slate and shown to the teacher. The teacher's work was to maintain order and to direct effort, rather than to hear pupils recite, and he strove to stimulate the children to make the best use of the short time they could attend school." —**Ellwood P. Cubberley**, *Rural Life and Education*, 1914, 88

ENGLISH TEACHERS

"If all teachers, both in elementary and in high schools, realized the importance of training pupils to talk well, every recitation would become an exercise in the use of good spoken English. Then there would be as vigorous criticism of English in arithmetic and geography as in language lessons, and nowhere in the school would slovenly English be tolerated. Every teacher would be a teacher of English." —**Calvin Kendall and George Mirick**, *How to Teach the Fundamental Subjects*, 1915, 68

THE FORGOTTEN TEACHER

"One of the most pathetic figures in all society is the teacher who has been lost in the system, save that he or she fits like a small cog in a vast machine and clicks automatically with the school clock. Her voice is never heard in the councils, her opinion is never asked, and her responses come only in reply to commands. Being subject to the order of the chief, she has been dwarfed into the form of a slave; she may develop all the tendencies of the slave and measure her labor by the rotation of the earth, and her efficiency and sense of responsibility to the community by the size of her pay check."
—**Eugene C. Brooks**, *Education for Democracy*, 1919, 75

THE GENERAL

"A teacher's task is much the same as that of a military general. If he has not a hostile army in front of him he, at any rate, has a body of children in more or less resistance to the things they ought to do. Now a good general plans the conditions of the battle. Nothing in the configuration of the ground and no obstructions to the movement of troops are overlooked. He tries to plan a situation, by means of the contour of the field and through obstacles to the movement of the opposing forces, that shall compel the enemy to do the things he wants them to do. In other words he forces adaption to the situation which he has planned; and he does it against the will of his opponents by utilizing conditions at his disposal and by creating others. Skill in this makes up his generalship." —**Edgar James Swift**, *Learning and Doing*, 1914, 190–91

GET A LIFE

"There is scarcely a calling which tends so to narrowness as does the teaching profession. In spite of a good education, of opportunities to travel, of more or less leisure, the earnest teacher is too often inclined to forget everything else and bury herself in her school work. It claims her first waking thought; she tells at the breakfast table what happened yesterday; she works legitimately in the school-room all morning. Usually she has her luncheon with other teachers, and the conversation is about Johnny or what was said in the class. The afternoon is a repetition of the morning from which the teacher carries home with her the nagging thought of something that has gone wrong. School thrusts itself into the dinner conversation. Papers to correct, lessons to look over for the morrow, fill up the dull evening which sends weary head to pillow, to thresh much of it all over again." —**Florence Milner**, *The Teacher*, 1912, 33

"Above all, the teacher must be careful not to take school with her when she finishes the work of the day. She is in a bad state if she gets to the point where she is eating, drinking, sleeping, and living school." —**Arthur C. Perry Jr.**, *Discipline as a School Problem*, 1915, 143

"A good daily program—For teaching, six hours; planning and preparing the lessons to be taught, three hours; meals, eating and healthful relaxation following, three hours; sleep, eight hours; resting, recreation, and exercise, two hours; –in all twenty-two hours. This leaves two hours each day which can be and should be used by the teacher for self-improvement. The teacher's program should devote these hours to reading and study with the same regularity and persistence as other hours are devoted to teaching, planning and preparing lessons, eating, sleeping, resting, and exercise, and nothing but dire necessity should be permitted to interfere with this program. Teachers, like all other individuals who desire to grow, must have a definite plan for reading and study, and they must stick to it." —**Oscar Corson**, *Our Public Schools: Their Teachers, Pupils, and Patrons*, 1918, 79–80

HEALTH

"The question of health is of greatest importance to the teacher. Impaired health means added effort and reduced usefulness. It is pathetic to see a teacher struggle on day after day, held by necessity to his work long after his efficiency is impaired and the joy of the work is gone. But the teacher is not the only sufferer. His pupils, too, suffer. They not only suffer intellectual loss from the reduced efficiency of the teacher, but they lose the inspiration and the gladness that flow from a teacher who has abundant physical energy." — **Charles McKenny**, *The Personality of the Teacher*, 1910, 171

HIGH SCHOOL TEACHERS

"In 1902 there were in the United States 6,292 Public Secondary Schools containing 550,611 students taught by 11,457 women and 10,958 men. According to Luckey and others who have carefully investigated the subject, these teachers have had no special training for their work. What they know about the psychology of development, about childhood and adolescence, whatever professional training they have acquired, they have gained from self-directed study and from their own experience. No special training is required. None is given save that inevitable training, good as far as it goes, which the inexperienced teacher always gets from the pupils themselves." — **William Book**, "The High School Teacher from the Pupil's Point of View," *Pedagogical Seminary* V (September 1905): 240

THE IDEAL TEACHER

"The ideal teacher is an intelligent, hard-working public servant, whose field of endeavor is limited only by the needs of the community which he serves. The number of teachers who have thus exalted the office of teacher in the community is happily increasing. The moral effect upon the lives of children of association with such a man or woman cannot be overestimated." — **George Strayer**, *A Brief Course in the Teaching Process*, 1911, 155

THE MEDIATOR

"[I]t is the task of the teacher to be the medium of communication between the pupil's mind and the subject-matter. Without him, it is dead stuff to them. He knows both them and it. From it he selects those things they can bear and them he gradually widens to cover it. Without him, they are self-taught, and so poorly taught; with him, their growth is consecutive and the subject appears in its intrinsic and extrinsic articulation. The teacher, between impersonal truth and personal life is the mediator." —**Herman Harrell Horne**, *The Psychological Principles of Education*, 1909, 39

MODELING

"First of all, the teacher's language should be good, grammatically correct, and worthy of imitation. This is of vital importance. The teacher's conversations with the children, her remarks to classes and to the school, are so many continuous lessons in language; they are more effective than all other lessons." —**Daniel Putnam**, *A Manual of Pedagogics*, 1899, 177

MOVIES

"The best schoolhouse is the screen, the best teacher is the film. Human teachers will be needed only to help guide and direct the minds of the pupils, but pictures will do the instructing. . . . The pupils will learn everything there is to learn, in every grade from the lowest to the highest. The long years now spent in cramming indigestible knowledge down unwilling young throats and in examining young minds on subjects which they can never learn under the present system, will be cut down marvelously, waste will be eliminated, and the youth of every land will at last become actually educated. If the Government should establish a film factory, with a special department for distribution on a small rental basis, and introduce such an educational system so as to pay minimum expenses, I venture to predict that it would bring about a revolutionary change for the better in our entire school organization. . . . The trouble now is that school is too dull; it holds no interest for the average boy or girl. It was so in my school-days and it has changed but little. But make every classroom and every assembly-hall a movie-show, a show where the child learns every moment while his eyes are glued to the screen, and you'll have one hundred per cent attention. Why, you won't be able to keep boys and girls away from school then. They'll get there ahead of time and scramble for good seats, and they'll stay late begging to see some of the films over again. I'd like to be a boy again when film-teaching becomes universal." — **Thomas Edison** as quoted in "Motion-Picture Schoolhouses to Prevent Future Wars," *Current Opinion*, 1919, 234–35

PATRIOTIC WORK

"There is no more patriotic work than [teaching]; for it is not amid the thunders of the battle-field, where men slay their fellow-men, that the noblest civic laurels are won, but in the quiet school-room, where devoted patriots, men and women, combine to slay misery, meanness, and corruption." — **Thomas Davidson**, *A History of Education*, 1900, 276

A PHILOSOPHY OF EDUCATION

"The greatest boon which a teacher can possess, for his peace of mind and his professional success, is a consistent philosophy of education, to which he has given his best thought and which rules his conduct. Such a philosophy will not be an unchanging belief, for experiences which are inconsistent with it will force the teacher to modify it. If he grows, it will become richer as he becomes older and wiser, but, as far as it goes, it fits his knowledge and experience. There are no spots of which he is aware which are mental aliens." —**William Stark**, *Every Teacher's Problems*, 1922, 357

POLITICAL INFLUENCE OF TEACHERS

"We are prone to bewail the fact that the opinion of educators has little weight in our legislative assemblies. This has been too true in the past. But this is due rather to the fact that teachers and school administrators as a rule have known so little of the temper of the people that the lawmakers, who are experienced politicians, are afraid to follow them. 'The people won't stand for it,' they say, and the educators are unable to answer them, for they do not know what the people will stand for." —**Eugene C. Brooks**, *Education for Democracy*, 1919, 112–13

THE REFLECTIVE TEACHER

"The best teachers make every recitation an examination in its truest sense. Such examine themselves more than their pupils. The questions they put to themselves are: 'What end shall I seek in this day's lesson?' 'What means shall I use in attainment of that end?' 'What contributed most to the success or failure of yesterday?' 'What have I reason to expect of my pupils as the result of their known ability?'" —**J. L. Pickard**, *School Supervision*, 1905, 100

"Classrooms have the right to be classrooms, with their own ways of doing things. They do not need to be like stores, nor offices, nor homes, but they can demonstrate in action the usual codes of polite intercourse and businesslike procedure. When the school day does not seem to be either polite or businesslike, a very old teacher's maxim may find useful application: 'If pupils happen to be particularly stupid, lazy, or ill mannered, ask *yourself* where *your* mistake is.'" —**S. E. Davis**, *The Teacher's Relationships*, 1930, 194–95

RESISTANCE TO CHANGE

"[T]here are teachers who have some good ways, but who are so prejudiced that they have no regard for anything outside their own work; they cling to the old, have a ready-made objection to the new, and have ceased to examine." —**Francis Parker**, *Talks on Teaching*, 1883, 16

"One would fancy that the school-teachers of Massachusetts, especially of the intelligent city of Boston, would have received him [Horace Mann] and his discoveries with open arms; but far from it. They denied *in toto* every proposition he made; they proved to their own satisfaction that that which he brought was nonsense; that their ways were the best ways; that the strap must be used; that the 'A, B, C's' must be taught; and that the children must go through the dreary round of oral spelling before they could learn to spell. The battle was a fierce and prolonged one: the people were aroused against innovations, and accused the children's champion of heresy and fanaticism." — **Francis Parker**, *Talks on Pedagogics*, 1894, 429

REWARDS FOR GOOD TEACHING

"There is a general conviction that the contrasts between teaching on the one hand and administration and supervision on the other hand have been too sharply drawn. In many cases, indeed, there has been no way in which to reward exceptionally meritorious teaching except to take the successful teacher from the classroom and from actual daily contact with boys and girls, and make of him or her a supervisory or administrative official." —**William Chandler Bagley and John Keith**, *An Introduction to Teaching*, 1929, 379

SOCIAL LIFE OF TEACHERS

"The teacher must remember that in so far as she conforms to the conventions of the community in which she lives, in so far as she avoids giving opportunity for adverse criticism, she will increase her prestige and power for effective work. In many communities she may find that her personal habits are subject to a particularly close scrutiny and rigid standards, but always she will be a thousand times repaid for creating for herself a favorable reputation among the people with whom she is to live and labor." —**J. Frank Marsh**, *The Teacher Outside the School*, 1928, 155

STRESS

"Teaching is a frightful strain. An overburdened curriculum, an unduly stimulating intellectual tonic, unreasonable financial demand, with the terrors of political interference, are a combination which may well make any teacher desperate." —**A. E. Winship**, "Professional Sentiment," *Addresses and Proceedings of the National Education Association*, 1899, 230

SUBSTITUTE TEACHING

"Substitute teaching is a difficult type of work. The teacher does not know the pupils, and so she cannot be familiar with their work. To a certain extent they are likely to resent the coming of a new teacher, and consequently may take advantage of her in every way they can. She will find the experience much like a succession of first days of schools. The better city school systems are at last realizing the unusual difficulties of the substitute, and are tending to appoint some of the strongest and most experienced teachers as regular substitutes, at higher salaries." —**John Almack and Albert Lang**, *The Beginning Teacher*, 1928, 17

SUPPORT FOR TEACHERS

"[I]t is the duty of the community to coöperate with the teacher for the furtherance of any plan which has for its purpose the improvement of school conditions and the best interests of the child. The community, and particularly the parents, should uphold the teacher's authority and acts so far as possible, and be very slow to criticize, even though the teacher may have done something which they do not understand or which they disapprove. If such a case occurs, it is better to investigate carefully, and if necessary talk with the teacher regarding it. Even though a teacher may have erred, it is neither wise nor just to advertise the matter and thereby lessen the value of his work and influence through open discussion and criticism. If parents and the community in general would observe proper ethical obligations toward the teachers in the schools and encourage them by giving them helpful coöperation and sympathy, the teachers would have more joy in the discharge of their duties, would put more heart into their work, and would achieve better results." —**O. I. Woodley and M. Virginia Woodley**, *The Profession of Teaching*, 1917, 21–22

TEACHER ATTITUDE

"We may well hold before us, in our teaching, strong, steady, quiet work as an ideal, and strive to make our practice attain it. The remedy lies largely, as does the fault, with the teacher herself. She can plunge her pupils into hurry and worry, or she can lead them through honest work into paths of peace. She can fasten their eyes upon the answer to the present problem, or make them glory in the conscious strength that comes of patient labor. She can choose patience instead of fretfulness, growth instead of per cents, cheerfulness instead of worry, vigor rather than excitement. The children will follow where she leads." —**Sarah Arnold**, *Waymarks for Teachers Showing Aims, Principles, and Plans of Everyday Teaching*, 1894, 247

TEACHER OF THE FUTURE

"The teacher of the future will think out from scientific principles the best way to teach a given child to subtract or divide, as the engineer thinks out the best way to bridge a given river or tunnel a given hill. The study of these principles and their applications will demand as great talents and as close application as the study of the principles upon which medical or engineering practice rests." —**E. L. Thorndike**, *Education: A First Book*, 1912, 258

TEACHER KNOWLEDGE OF SUBJECT MATTER

"Even, then, to teach a small thing well we must be large. I asked a teacher what her subject was, and she answered, 'Arithmetic in the third grade.' But where is third grade found? In knowledge, or in the schools? Unhappily it is in the schools. But if one would be a teacher of arithmetic, it must be arithmetic she teaches and not third grade at all. We cannot accept these artificial bounds without damage." —**George Herbert Palmer**, *The Ideal Teacher*, 1908, 17–18

TEACHER MOOD

"The teacher's manner . . . is usually persistent. There is a manner which varies with the mood. Bright and sunny one day, perhaps because of special rest or unusual health, the teacher inspires her class and all goes well. Hurt, sad, or depressed some other day, from causes outside the schoolroom, she shares her depression with the pupils, and all goes wrong. She is happy, and the children sing, mistakes seem trivial, faults are lightly reproved. Her head aches, and she is weary; the classes are dull, errors abound and are inexcusable, and offences are severely punished. Her spirits are buoyant, and the work goes on wings; she is heavy-hearted, and the school is a dead weight." —**Sarah Arnold**, *Waymarks for Teachers Showing Aims, Principles, and Plans of Everyday Teaching*, 1894, 238–39

TEACHER SCHOLARSHIP

"A teacher needs to be a student of live issues. Needs to read and study the best things being done in the best things being done in the best way this year. Every teacher needs to see how live teachers are doing live things to-day.

Every teacher needs to read about the real achievements of really vitalizing teachers with the most vital problems of to-day." —**A. E. Winship**, *Danger Signals for Teachers*, 1919, 62

"Every teacher should know more than he teaches. The youngest pupil in kindergarten knows enough to appreciate the fact that no one should attempt to teach what he does not understand. Adequate scholarship for the preparation of teaching should go beyond the subjects to be taught and take account of those subjects which are related to them. This is absolutely necessary in order to know what to emphasize and what to neglect in the subjects to be taught. . . . Adequate scholarship makes possible a breadth of view and a keen appreciation of the things we are doing." —**George Frasier and Winfred Armentrout**, *An Introduction to Education*, 1924, 13

TEACHER STATUS

"[T]he present status of the American teacher is this: He has limited but rather definite legal authority with its attendant responsibility; he has practically no official standing; he is but poorly remunerated financially; and his social and professional standing depend almost wholly upon his personal qualities and little upon the legal recognition of his calling. And yet we are conscious day by day of a gain; we may be confident that the teacher's status of a generation hence will be far in advance of that of to-day." —**Arthur C. Perry**, *The Status of the Teacher*, 1912, 59–60

TEACHER TEMPERAMENT

"Any prominent displays of swagger and self-conceit operate against the teacher's influence, and incite efforts to take him down. It is possible to temper authority with an unassuming demeanour." —**Alexander Bain**, *Education as a Science*, 1896, 110

TEACHER TURNOVER

"If public education is to prosper there must be a permanent teaching class with well defined traditions, rights, prerogatives, and duties, and the members of this class must not only maintain their own self-respect, but must secure public respect; they must constitute one of the learned professions and as such must inherit and transmit all that is implied in professional spirit and standing. I sharply distinguish teachers of this class from accidental, provisional, or non-professional teachers, those who teach for a term or a year through caprice or necessity, without any special competency, and then pass to some regular employment. Money spent on such teachers is in the main wasted." —**W. H. Payne**, *The Education of Teachers*, 1901, 52

"The 'average life' of the elementary teacher is certainly not more than four years, and this means that approximately one half of all those entering the teaching service leave this service before they have reached their fifth year of experience." —**William Chandler Bagley**, *School Discipline*, 1915, 25

TEACHERS

"But the one truth that demands first and strongest emphasis is *the vital need of proper qualifications in the teacher.* Other things may be important, this is essential. The teacher is the soul of his measures. If he is weak, they will be weak; if he is strong in personal resources, they will be potent. The vital factor in a school is the teacher. He is cause; all else is only condition and result." —**Emerson E. White**, *School Management*, 1893, 19

"There is no higher work than teaching; and he who does not appreciate this truth, who does not love to see [the] mind grow and to help it grow and know, has no rightful place in the ranks of those who are consecrating the schools to the cause of humanity." —**Ruric Roark**, *Psychology in Education*, 1895, 283

"The great need of teachers is vision, broad and accurate; a discriminating outlook upon the drama of existence as it portrays the struggle of the race upwards towards the light." —**W. H. Payne**, *The Education of Teachers*, 1901, 24

"Direct contact with a noble-hearted teacher is worth more to the feelings of pupils than all precepts put together. Pupils, so to say, absorb the feelings of the teacher, and drift into his current. It must therefore be important that the teacher cultivate propriety and vigor of feeling in himself, not only for his own sake, but also for absorption by his pupils." —**Charles Boyer**, *Principles and Methods of Teaching*, 1902, 86

"There are persons who, with all good will, can never be teachers. They are not made in that way. Their business it is to pry into knowledge, to engage in action, to make money, or to pursue whatever other aim their powers dictate; but they do not readily think in terms of the other person. They should not, then, be teachers." —**George Herbert Palmer**, *The Ideal Teacher*, 1908, 14

"But, when all is said and done, the fact remains that some teachers have a naturally inspiring presence, and can make their exercises interesting, while others simply cannot. And psychology and general pedagogy here confess their failure, and hand things over to the deeper springs of human personality to conduct the task." —**William James**, *Talks to Teachers*, 1910, 105–6

"A true teacher is never merely teaching a subject. He is always assisting a human being by means of a subject to grow and adapt himself to his surroundings. It is then, after all, the pupils' interest, success, growth, improvement that the teacher has in mind when he sets high standards and puts into operation stimulating incentives." —**Calvin Kendall and George Mirick**, *How to Teach the Fundamental Subjects*, 1915, 103

"It is exceedingly unfortunate for any community in its employment of teachers to proceed upon the theory that a high degree of technical skill in classroom instruction is unnecessary or unimportant so long as pupils are in charge of good and intelligent persons. Great skill in the technique of instruction is absolutely required of every teacher if the school is to do its work well. Not every beginner can be an expert instructor, but no one preparing to teach should for a moment lose sight of the fact that skillful *teaching* is the distinguishing mark of every one who has a moral right to be in charge of a classroom." —**S. E. Davis**, *The Work of the Teacher*, 1918, 139

THEORY INTO PRACTICE

"What college men want in a course in principles of education is first sound practice, and then only enough theory to understand it." —**Herman Herrell Horne**, "Commentary in John MacVannel," *The College Course in the Principles of Education*, 1906, 51

"Every year we have thousands of young teachers who are asking to be guided from the land of theory into the land of practice. The passage across this borderland is the most difficult thing in education, and, to say the least, the leaders of American education are not skillful in inducting young people, by their own example, into skillful classroom work." —**Charles McMurry**, *Conflicting Principles in Teaching*, 1914, 248

TYPES OF TEACHERS WHO FAIL

"Here is a list of ten types of teachers who can hardly hope to succeed:

1. The teacher too ignorant and crude to command the respect of students.

2. The conceited or bigoted teacher, whose pretensions or narrowness provoke their derision.
3. The weak-willed teacher.
4. The teacher ignorant of working devices [techniques for how to manage students].
5. The teacher whose life outside the schoolroom does not command the respect of pupils or townspeople.
6. The teacher who descends to the level of his pupils, treating them with easy levity and familiarity; *and the gossip*.
7. The taskmaster and the tyrant.
8. The teacher who wants, above everything else, to be popular.
9. The lazy teacher.
10. The threatener who does not 'make good.'"

—**Frances Morehouse**, *The Discipline of the School*, 1914, 219–20

"Unfortunately, there is a type of teacher in the schools, that follows the line of least resistance, that does what he finds easiest to do, that follows mechanical routine, that could not deviate from this fixed orbit any more than could the mechanical toy. The springs of his being seem to be cast in an inflexible mould as is the spring that controls the motions of the toy. He teaches as well this year as last, but will teach no better next year than he did two years ago; in fact, he gradually deteriorates with age as he does not have within himself the power to be rejuvenated. It is this static teacher who is the millstone about the neck of our educational system." —**C. R. Maxwell**, *The Observation of Teaching*, 1917, 38

"The typically poor teacher has poor discipline; is incapable of stimulating interest; and makes no provision for individual differences. She follows a textbook assignment and organization of subject matter; provides formal textbook teaching, and makes little effort to socialize class discussions. The poor teacher appraises the pupils' responses but possesses few commentarial remarks for this purpose. She may be lazy; she may loaf or she may bluff; she may nag her pupils, show favoritism, or be too familiar with the boys in her class. Some poor teachers are sarcastic, some dictatorial, and some indifferent. The list of weaknesses shown by poor teachers is a long one." —**A. S. Barr**, *Characteristic Differences of Good and Poor Teachers*, 1929, 115–16

"Why do communities ask teachers to leave? Some of the reasons are:
"Poor discipline
"Poor knowledge of subject matter
"Lack of instructional skill
"Inability to cooperate
"Indiscreet conduct socially." —**S. E. Davis**, *The Teacher's Relationships*, 1930, 76

THE WISE TEACHER

"The wise teacher often shuts her eyes to misdemeanors which would be emphasized by open reproof. The attention of the school is attracted by the reprimand to faults which otherwise they would never see. If the teacher is constantly calling for order, the pupils become impressed with the fact that the school is disorderly, and that the teacher cannot help it. A quiet word to the offender, a look or sign, a conversation after school when nobody else knows, are better than the open correction. They do not arouse the spirit of defiance as does the open reproof. The teacher's manner in necessary direction, should assume the intention to obey, not antagonism. Her attitude toward the child does much to determine his own. Anticipating obedience and good will, she will find them; looking for malice and mutiny, she will doubtless discover them likewise." —**Sarah Arnold**, *Waymarks for Teachers Showing Aims, Principles, and Plans of Everyday Teaching*, 1894, 270

WORKING CONDITIONS OF TEACHERS

"No indiscriminate allegations are made against the teachers of the city schools. As a class, they are worthy, industrious, and conscientious. The conditions under which they work make life hard. Ordinarily, it is mechanical and monotonous. It seldom rises above the commonplace. They are lectured to and kept under edicts and rules until the spirit breaks. Most of them would be glad to advance, and would advance, if there were opportunity and anything to inspire them; but such is not the case. With exceptions so rare that they do not count, the teachers in the elementary schools of all the greater American cities are tramping around in small circles which are very nearly on the same plane; and the schools do little more than mark time in endless routine." —**A. S. Draper**, "Common Schools in the Larger Cities," *The Forum* VII (June 1899): 390

Chapter Sixteen

Teaching Methods

One of the first observations made about teaching was that teachers teach the way they were taught. Teachers were cautioned that telling is not teaching and that there was no one teaching method to fit all children. Introducing new material must begin from what the student knows to what is new, and what the student knows must come from the student's everyday world. Educators advocated discovery as the best teaching method; however there are times when direct instruction may be necessary or desired.

As early as the 1840s there was a mistrust new educational innovations. Teachers learned quickly there were frequent attempts to introduce teaching fads and gimmicks in place of time tested teaching methods, and that they should be aware of how superficial many innovations can be. Finally, Judd complained that American education was highly dependent on the overuse of textbooks while European education (often viewed as superior to American education) relied on the expertise of the teacher as the major source of information.

HEURISTIC METHOD

"In the heuristic method the plan is to induce the student to find out for himself, instead of telling him the answers to his problems. The purpose is to constantly shift the activity from teacher to student, thus creating the atmosphere of discovery. The leading merit of this method is its emphasis on the activity and initiative secured on the part of the student, and is thus a reaction against the too common fault of doing for the student what the student should learn to do for himself." —**Herbert Foster**, *Principles of Teaching in Secondary Education*, 1921, 121

IDEAL INSTRUCTION

"We shall probably never be able to dispense wholly with direct instruction in dealing with learners, and yet ideal instruction must be causative rather than communicative, *i.e.*, the process of instruction must consist of assignments, stimuli, and supervision rather than of telling, stating, imparting, etc. To cause the learner to think is the distinctive purpose of modern instruction." —**Charles C. Boyer**, *Modern Methods for Teachers*, 1908, 44

INNOVATIONS

"It [is] unreasonable to expect that the difficulties of education are to be surmounted without some abortive dangerous innovations and extremes. But the precipitous movements of the present age seem to have multiplied them to an extraordinary degree; insomuch that we rest not upon one point long enough to make a fair experiment, before we fly to another. Indeed innovation seems to be the prevailing spirit of our age." —**Hubbard Winslow**, "The Dangerous Tendency to Innovations and Extremes in Education," *Proceedings of the American Institute of Instruction*, 1834, 169

"Listening merely to the noise that is made in the educational world by the loud-voiced and not overmodest reformer, we might conclude that the school is in a very bad way, that nothing has really been settled in the way of principles and methods, but that the whole scholastic *régime* is to be created *de novo*. A striking phenomenon of the times is a rapid succession of educational fads, some philosophical, some methodical, some enduring for a season, others disappearing after a fitful effort to maintain an existence." —**W. H. Payne**, *The Education of Teachers*, 1901, 109

"It is true that supervisors, being human, sometimes trail after fleeting catch-words of current pedagogy. Where this happens once, teachers probably make the accusation of 'fad methods' ten times. Most supervisors know that reforms of method are oftener superficial waves than deep currents, and that the whole of expert schoolroom practice cannot be compressed into a single formula." —**S. E. Davis**, *The Teacher's Relationships*, 1930, 140

INTRODUCING NEW MATERIAL

"It is evident enough that the material of instruction for the first years of school life should be selected from the child's immediate surroundings. It does not matter much what name is given to this material. It may be called 'elementary science' or whatever one prefers, provided only the thing itself is secured. Such selection of material enables the school and the teacher to meet the child on familiar ground. He is prepared to apperceive or assimilate the subject-matter presented to him. The school is not a new and unknown world, but rather a continuation of the world in which he has been living." — **Daniel Putnam**, *A Manual of Pedagogics*, 1899, 160

"[T]he teacher cannot hypodermically inject new subject-matter into the pupil. He can move forward only in so far as problems of development emerge within the capital that he has. If they do not arise within this subject-matter, the thing which the teacher thinks he is teaching slides off the child's experience like water off the proverbial duck's back. Each branch of subject-matter grows just as the individual grows, by the development of what he already has." —**W. W. Charters**, *Methods of Teaching*, 1912, 221

LEARNING FROM TEACHING

"Nearly all beginners who ranked high in scholarship at graduation discover that, after all, they do not know much about the subjects in which they have passed examinations and earned high marks. Those who ranked low and barely made the required averages are likely to find themselves much worse off, if they succeed in finding themselves at all. A huge amount of study is necessitated the first time one teaches a grade or subject. The teacher who says, 'I learned more than any of my pupils did,' is stating the case conservatively. In this, reference is made only to increased knowledge of subject matter, not to the unpaid debt to pupils for what they have taught the teacher." —**S. E. Davis**, *The Teacher's Relationships*, 1930, 173–74

TEACHING METHODS

"Teachers have been content to follow the methods in which they themselves were taught." —**James Johonnot**, *Principles and Practice of Teaching*, 1881, 51

"In all teaching the maxim, '*Proceed from the known to the unknown*' rightly interpreted, should be regarded. The maxim may be understood to mean this: when presenting a new subject or a new lesson to a child, make what the child already knows the starting-point, and from this lead him, by natural and easy steps, to grasp and master the new, the now unknown thing. The known, selected as the point of departure, should be chosen with careful reference to some obvious relation existing between it and the unknown thing which is to be learned." —**Daniel Putnam**, *A Manual of Pedagogics*, 1899, 142

"Whether a teacher's methods shall be inspiring and creative, or obstructive and deadening will depend on whether, to borrow Carlyle's imagery, he is a live coal or a dead cinder; and it is necessary to be kept in mind that in some way a student must be transformed into a quickening spirit before he can become a real teacher. In a school devoted to the education of teachers there must be a prevalent spirit provocative of high moral aims, devotion to duty and love of the scholarly vocation. This spirit should be so prevalent and so tonic as to form the vital breath of every learner; it should be so effective that it can be felt as a living, vitalizing power where-ever students congregate—in chapel, in classrooms, in lecture halls, in art rooms, in library, everywhere." —**W. H. Payne**, *The Education of Teachers*, 1901, 34

"[N]ew methods of teaching have not entirely replaced the older and harsher methods. There are frequently points at which pulling and guiding must give place to prodding. It is safe to say that the point will never be reached where pain and drudgery can be entirely eliminated from the educative process." —**William Chandler Bagley**, *The Educative Process*, 1908, 113

"There can be no itemized method of pedagogy that will be of universal application to all children of all the people. We can get 'helps and hints' from a thousand and one sources. But the whole business can never be put into a book, neither can it be gotten out of a book. Here is a place where manipulation can only be partially transmitted. The ultimate art must be individually acquired, and personally exercised; and neither acquirement nor exercise can be obtained without practice upon the real thing, with flesh and blood children. That is the final word about methods in teaching." —**William Hawley Smith**, *All the Children of All the People*, 1912, 312

"One very impressive difference between the schools of the United States and the schools of Europe is to be found in the fact that class exercises in our schools are commonly based on assignments in textbooks, while in Europe the chief method of instruction is oral exposition by the teacher. The word 'recitation,' which is often employed in describing a classroom exercise, is an American term. It originated at the period when devotion to the textbook was even greater than it is now,–when the pupil was expected to repeat verbatim the passage from the text. In British books on education the word 'recitation' appears only when referring to American practices, and usually takes the form 'the American recitation.' In the German educational vocabulary the word has no equivalent." —**Charles Judd**, *Introduction to the Scientific Study of Education*, 1918, 14–15

TELLING VS. TEACHING

"The commonest error of the gifted scholar, inexperienced in teaching, is to expect pupils to know what they have been told. But telling is not teaching. The expression of the facts that are in one's mind is a natural impulse when one wishes others to know these facts, just as to cuddle and pat a sick child is a natural impulse. But telling a fact to a child may not cure his ignorance of it any more than patting him will cure his scarlet fever." —**E. L. Thorndike**, *Education: A First Book*, 1912, 61

Chapter Seventeen

Testing

Perhaps today's educators can relate most to what was written about the standard course of study and overuse of testing in the period leading up to the twentieth century. Parker complained that the standard course of study required teachers to set a fast pace so as to keep the testing on schedule; he felt that teaching was being replaced by testing. There were concerns about the emotional effect testing had on students, and that teachers were not to deviate from the standard course of study.

Teachers believed they could not individualize instruction because the teacher's job was to prepare students for the frequent tests students had to pass. White said that using tests to determine achievement differences among children and schools was an abuse of testing.

Critics of testing thought that education had become simply a process where children were required to memorize large amounts of information so they could perform well on tests. For many, the over-emphasis on testing that drove much of the school reform movement prior to the twentieth century has returned as a dominate force in the twenty-first century.

COLLEGE ENTRANCE EXAMS

"Whatever be the subject, our teachers will gain greatly by forgetting, as far as possible, that bane of education, the entrance examination for college. After all possible arguments in its defense, it still remains true that this examination is the strongest possible incentive to the memorizing of words, rules, exceptions, and other disconnected facts. The cramming process is the foe of genuine thinking. The colleges and universities have wisely broadened the field of studies which will prepare for entrance. They will broaden it still more. The amount of material which must be learned or surveyed as a preparation may be, and probably is, larger than the schools can handle in the time at their disposal consistently with the best mental growth and discipline." — **John Mason Tyler**, *Growth and Education*, 1907, 189–90

INSTRUCTION DRIVEN BY TESTS

"The testimony of countless good teachers has been uniform in this respect. When asked, 'Why don't you do better work? Why don't you use the methods taught in the normal schools, and advocated by educational periodicals and books?' the answer is, 'We cannot do it. Look at our course of study. In three weeks, or months, these children will be examined. We have not one moment of time to spend in real teaching!' No wonder that teaching is a trade, and not an art!" —**Francis Parker**, *Talks on Teaching*, 1883, 152

INTELLECTUAL BLINDERS

"Exorbitant desire for uniformity of procedure and for prompt external results are the chief foes which the open-minded attitude meets in school. The teacher who does not permit and encourage diversity of operation in dealing with questions is imposing intellectual blinders upon pupils—restricting their vision to the one path the teacher's mind happens to approve. Probably the chief cause of devotion to rigidity of methods is, however, that it seems to promise speedy, accurately measurable, correct results. The zeal for 'answers' is the explanation of much of the zeal for rigid and mechanical methods." —**John Dewey**, *Democracy and Education*, 1916, 206

INTELLIGENCE TESTING

"It is safe to predict that in the near future intelligence tests will bring tens of thousands of . . . high-grade defectives under the surveillance and protection of society. This will ultimately result in curtailing the reproduction of feeble-mindedness and in the elimination of an enormous amount of crime, pauperism, industrial inefficiency." —**Lewis Terman**, *The Measurement of Intelligence*, 1916, 7

"[T]he common opinion that the child from a cultured home does better in tests solely by reason of his superior home advantages is an entirely gratuitous assumption. Practically all of the investigations which have been made of the influence of nature and nurture on mental performance agree in attributing far more to original endowment than to environment. Common observation would itself suggest that the social class to which the family belongs depends less on chance than on the parents' native qualities of intellect and character." —**Lewis Terman**, *The Measurement of Intelligence*, 1916, 115

MEASURING RESULTS

"Our aim should be to accomplish results with the smallest possible expenditure of nervous force on the part of both teacher and pupil; to give the teacher all possible freedom within certain limits; to judge of intellectual work by intellectual, not mechanical, tests; and to train our children to move forward, not like an army at the word of command, every soldier drilled to the exact similitude of every other soldier, not like the cataract, beautiful, but tumultuous and destructive, but like a flock of swallows, rejoicing in their liberty and ever flying to the promised land." —**W. H. Maxwell**, "Examinations as Tests for Promotion," *Journal of Proceedings and Addresses of the National Education Association*, 1890, 137

"Teachers, more than most workers, must remember that the results of much of their work are placed in the invisible future, requiring us to toil by faith. Teachers would do well, however, to measure their work by whatever evidences are apparent that they are helping some person to overcome resistance—to overcome obstacles to progress toward usefulness and happiness."
—**J. Frank Marsh**, *The Teacher Outside the School*, 1928, 100–1

SCHOOL EXAMINATIONS

"Those who understand children will readily appreciate the excitement and strain under which they labor when their fate depends upon the correct answering of ten disconnected questions. It is well known to you that some of the best pupils generally do their worst in the confusion that attends such highly wrought nervous states. How much better, then, is it to take the entire work of the pupil for the whole year than the results of one hour under such adverse conditions?" —**Francis Parker**, *Talks on Teaching*, 1883, 150

"School examinations should give a systematic, accurate and fairly complete account of the pupil's knowledge of school subjects but they fail to give any estimate of what a child knows about common things, and they do not prove that he has a clear idea because he uses the proper words in a correct answer." —**Arthur Holmes**, *Backward Children*, 1915, 195–96

Chapter 17
TESTS AND TESTING

"The test has been widely abused in American schools, and this abuse has had an unfavorable influence, especially on elementary education. . . . The use of examination results as a means of comparing the standing of schools and pupils has narrowed and made mechanical the instruction of many . . . teachers capable of better work. It is indeed, difficult to determine which is the greater evil, the use of improper tests or the improper use of test results."
—**Emerson E. White**, *The Elements of Pedagogy*, 1886, 148

"'My success as a teacher is measured by the per cent of correct answers my pupils give to a series of questions submitted in the examinations for promotion to the high school. Whatever qualifications these tests call for I must produce or fail. I can not stop to inquire whether my instruction is right or wrong. *I must prepare my wares for the market.*'" —Principal of a grammar school, quoted by **Emerson E. White**, *The Elements of Pedagogy*, 1886, 201

"The nature of the tests given by many teachers, as well as their teaching, shows that their principal aim is for objective results—for the mere memorizing of facts, rather than for subjective results, as shown in the acquisition of clear concepts and the right exercise of the reasoning powers. By an objective result is meant the ability on the part of the child to report an answer to questions asked, the information received from study or from instruction. A child having a good memory may give back in reply to questions much information relating to the subject studied and yet have made little or no advancement in the acquisition of right concepts and in the power to think."
—**O. I Woodley and M. Virginia Woodley**, *The Profession of Teaching*, 1917, 144

"The teacher's work in 1920, as measured by tests, has been cross-sectioned, dissected, analyzed, and held up to public comment, often to scorn and ridicule. It is true that the results of modern tests have been a surprise to all, even to the teachers themselves. The scores made by children are ridiculously low, the individual variation enormous, the progress from year to year much smaller than expected and supposed to exist. The greatest chagrin from the situation has come from the frequent and uncomplimentary comparisons with the past. Parents have not hesitated to say: 'When we went to school, teaching was more effective.' 'In the good old days of drill and discipline, the children really learned something.' 'We learned when I was in school.' Parents and the public generally have not only said these things, they have believed them, and have blamed teachers and schoolmen generally for 'new-fangled methods' although the same have been developed with the intent and for the purpose of making the schools better." —**Otis W. Caldwell and Stuart A. Courtis**, *Then & Now in Education 1845:1923*, 1925, 47

"Although the development of instruments for the measurement of school products has had scientific as well as practical motive, its major claim for popular support has been made in the name of efficiency. When the movement was in its first flush of youth its champions advanced the most extreme claims regarding its practical utility. Many school administrators and students of education apparently believed that measurement held the key to the solution of all educational problems. Through the use of standardized tests they argued that systems, schools, teachers, and methods could be appraised. An era of rapid and uninterrupted educational advance consequently seemed immediately ahead. The result was an orgy of testing that swept through the entire country." —**George Counts**, *The American Road to Culture*, 1930, 148

Epilogue

The purpose of this book is not to suggest that schools have not changed; that the schools of today are similar to those of the past. Twenty-first century schools are very different from early twentieth-century schools. What remains constant is the rhetoric about what schools need to do to fulfill their mission to be democratic.

The question of how the schools could serve the educational needs of all students and at the same time provide all students with the skills and competencies to become equal participants in a democratic society has never been satisfactorily answered. Schools that admit all students regardless of their differences struggle with issues of how to provide an educational experience that motivates all children and also provides society with a highly educated citizenry.

Two distinct philosophic positions have tried to resolve the issue of how to provide a quality education for every student. The Progressive movement proposed that the interests and things of importance to students should form the basis of the curriculum. That is, the curriculum should arise from within the student.

Essentialism, based in the Social Efficiency movement, argued for a curriculum that would give all children the same essential information. The Essentialist curriculum could be delivered as a standard course of study from which all children were to learn the same core competencies and skills. This curriculum, they contended, would give all children an equal education. The standard course of study was often driven by college and university entrance requirements.

Regardless of which of these philosophic positions the schools took, educators confronted new and difficult challenges as the schools worked to create classrooms that could accommodate all children. The professional literature that grew between the years 1880 and 1935 document these challenges. What the literature often described was the chasm between the idealism of what *should be* to make schools work well and the realities of how schools actually operated.

The purpose of this book was to harvest some of the advice early education writers produced in the professional literature about how to create effective school and classroom practices; particularly practices for inclusive schools. The advice that was selected included topics that are still relevant in education today.

The constant theme in this early literature is that school reform is always imminent; it sits on the horizon. Depending on the political climate and who is in charge of legislatures, schools will be subject to new changes that will require educators to become more accountable. It is these reform efforts that influence classroom practices.

The literature tells us that in order to achieve new school reforms teachers must be given the respect and the acknowledgment that their work is hard and constantly demanding. It is honorable work that requires support from parents and the community. The role of administrators is to prepare the way for teachers to do the work they know how to do and boards of education must learn not to micromanage the classroom or interfere with the daily operations of the schools.

Students need challenging and stimulating classroom experiences that have personal relevance. Parents are to assist teachers and students are to arrive at school ready to learn. Teachers must accept children from where they are when they enter the classroom and help them to grow as students.

There are children who chronically misbehave in the classroom. Teachers who are successful managing students understand that misbehavior is often a symptom of a larger issue rather than a personal attack. There are alternatives to physical punishments.

Current standard classroom practices have not always been so accepting of this early educational wisdom. For example, there have been long-standing debates about the value of writing lesson plans. Lesson plans written for an administrator or supervisor are not the same as teachers planning for instruction. Lesson plans fit a format that needs to be approved by someone outside the classroom. Similarly, there have been debates about the value of homework.

The school curriculum seems to be always expanding. Rarely is something removed even though there may be questions of its relevancy. There have also been constant tensions in the curriculum between subjects that are school subjects (academic subjects) and life subjects (life skills).

There are early writings about the placement of exceptional children. Inclusive schools have a place for children with all sorts of disabilities. The recognition of the potential of exceptional children and the realities of providing an appropriate placement has taken almost a century to resolve, and there is still more work to do in this area.

Prospective teachers must have rigorous preparation to become effective classroom teachers. Much has been written throughout the twentieth century about how easy it was to become a teacher. This was particularly true in times of teacher shortages. High preparation standards vary with supply and demand. The uncertified lateral entry teacher is not a recent or new phenomenon.

Much was said about teaching methods. As early as 1899 there were questions about the value of direct instruction. Teachers were advised to use instructional methods that engaged the learner. Teachers were to assess what students knew so that new material could be integrated into the student's knowledge base.

Finally, early writers were concerned about the overuse of tests and the abuses related to using test results to compare the learning of children. Tests were tools for assessing progress, not for defining what an education is. The concern was that testing was replacing teaching, a charge that is still relevant in today's literature.

Sources

Almack, John C. and Albert Lang. *The Beginning Teacher.* Boston: Houghton Mifflin Company, 1928.
Arnold, Felix. *Attention and Interest: A Study in Psychology and Education.* New York: The Macmillan Company, 1910.
Arnold, Sarah L. *Waymarks for Teachers Showing Aims, Principles, and Plans of Everyday Teaching.* New York: Silver, Burdett, & Company, 1894.
Ayres, Leonard P. *Laggards in Our Schools: A Study of Retardation and Elimination in City School Systems.* New York: The Russell Sage Foundation, 1909.
Bagley, William Chandler. "Adolescence," in *Public School Methods*, vol. 6. Chicago: School Methods Company, Inc., 1921.
———. *Classroom Management.* New York: The Macmillan Company, 1911.
———. *The Educative Process.* New York: The Macmillan Company, 1908.
———. *School Discipline.* New York: The Macmillan Company, 1915.
Bagley, William Chandler and John Keith. *An Introduction to Teaching.* New York: The Macmillan Company, 1929.
Bain, Alexander. *Education as a Science.* New York: D. Appleton and Company, 1896.
Barr, Arvil S. *Characteristic Differences of Good and Poor Teachers.* Bloomington, Illinois: Public School Publishing Company, 1929.
Barr, Arvil S. and William Burton. *The Supervision of Instruction.* New York: D. Appleton and Company, 1926.
Benson, Arthur F. "The Present Status of the Junior High School." *Proceedings of the National Education Association* (1920): 528–31.
Bennett, Henry E. *School Posture and Seating.* Boston: Ginn and Company, 1928.
Betts, George H. *Social Principles of Education.* New York: Charles Scribner's Sons 1912.
Betts, George H. and Otis E. Hall. *Better Rural Schools.* Indianapolis: The Bobbs-Merrill Company, 1914.
Bobbitt, J. Franklin. *The Curriculum.* Cambridge: The Riverside Press, 1918.
———. *How to Make a Curriculum.* Cambridge: The Riverside Press, 1924.
Bonser, Frederick G. *The Elementary School Curriculum.* New York: The Macmillan Company, 1922.
Book, William F. "The High School Teacher from the Pupil's Point of View." *Pedagogical Seminary* V (September 1905): 239–88.
Boone, Richard. *Education in the United States.* New York: D. Appleton and Company, 1893.
Bowden, A. O. "Our 396 Major Social Problems and Issues and the Schools." *The Journal of Educational Sociology* (March, 1929): 397–411. Reprinted in E. George Payne, ed. *Readings in Educational Sociology.* New York: Prentice-Hall, 1934.

Boyer, Charles C. *Modern Methods for Teachers.* Philadelphia: J.B. Lippincott Company, 1908.

———. *Principles and Methods of Teaching.* Philadelphia: J.B. Lippincott Company, 1902.

Briggs, Thomas H. *The Junior High School.* Boston: Houghton, Mifflin, & Company, 1920.

Briggs, Thomas H. and Lotus D. Coffman. *Reading in Public Schools.* Chicago: Row, Peterson & Co., 1911.

Brooks, Eugene C. *Education for Democracy.* Chicago: Rand McNally & Company 1919.

Butler, Nicholas M. *The Meaning of Education.* New York: The Macmillan Company, 1903.

Caldwell, Otis W. "The Laboratory Method." *Popular Science Monthly* LXX (March 1913): 243-51.

Caldwell, Otis W. and Stuart A. Courtis. *Then & Now in Education 1845:1923.* Yonkers-on-Hudson, New York: World Book Company, 1925. Reprinted in Lawrence Cremin, ed. *American Education: Its Men, Ideas, and Institutions.* New York: Arno Press, 1971.

Cary, Edward. "An Evil of the Schools." *The Forum*, VI (June 1887): 417-22.

Chapman, J. Crosby and George S. Counts. *Principles of Education.* Boston: Houghton Mifflin Company, 1924.

Charters, W. W. *Curriculum Construction.* New York: The Macmillan Company, 1923.

———. *Methods of Teaching: Their Basis and Statement Developed from a Functional Standpoint.* Chicago: Row, Peterson & Company, 1912.

———. *The Teaching of Ideals.* New York: The Macmillan Company, 1928.

Clark, S. H. *How to Teach Reading in the Public Schools.* Chicago: Scott, Foresman and Company, 1898.

Colvin, Stephen S. and William Chandler Bagley. *Human Behavior: A First Book in Psychology for Teachers.* New York: The Macmillan Company, 1921.

Corson, Oscar T. *Our Public Schools: Their Teachers, Pupils, and Patrons.* New York: American Book Company, 1918.

Counts, George S. *The American Road to Culture.* New York: John Day, 1930.

———. *Dare the School Build a New Social Order?* New York: John Day, 1932.

Crawford, Claude C. *The Technique of Study.* Boston: Houghton Mifflin Company, 1928.

Cubberley, Elwood P. "A Distinctive American Achievement." *Educational Progress,* monograph, 5, no 2. Boston: Houghton Mifflin Company, 1926.

———. *Rural Life and Education.* Boston: Houghton Mifflin Company: Boston, 1914

———. *The Principal and His School.* Boston: Houghton Mifflin Company, 1923.

Davenport, Eugene. *Education for Efficiency.* Boston: D. C. Heath & Co., Publishers, 1914.

Davis, Sheldon E. *The Teacher's Relationships.* New York: The Macmillan Company, 1930.

———. *The Technique of Teaching.* New York: The Macmillan Company, 1924.

———. *The Work of the Teacher.* New York: The Macmillan Company, 1918.

Davidson, Thomas. *A History of Education.* New York: Charles Scribner's Sons, 1900.

Dearborn, Ned H. *An Introduction to Teaching.* New York: D. Appleton and Company, 1925.

DeGarmo, Charles. *Herbart and the Herbartians.* New York: Charles Scribner's Sons, 1895.

———. *Principles of Secondary Education.* New York: The Macmillan Company, 1909.

Dewey, John. *Democracy and Education.* New York: The Macmillan Company, 1916.

———. *How We Think.* Boston: D. C. Heath & Co., 1910.

———. "My Pedagogical Creed." *The School Journal* 54 (January 1897): 77–80.

———. *Moral Principles in Education.* Boston: Houghton Mifflin Company, 1909.

———. "The Relation of Theory to Practice in Education." *The Third Yearbook of the National Society for the Scientific Study of Education, Part I.* Chicago, 1904.

Dewey, John and Evelyn Dewey. *Schools of To-morrow.* New York: E.P. Dutton & Co., 1915.

Draper, Andrew S. "Common Schools in the Larger Cities." *The Forum* VII (June 1899): 385–97.

Dutton, Samuel T. *School Management.* New York: Charles Scribner's Sons, 1903.

Earhart, Lida B. *Types of Teaching.* Boston: Houghton Mifflin 1915.

Ellis, William J. "Physically and Mentally Handicapped Children: A Program for Their Adjustment." *The Journal of Educational Sociology* (February 1932): 368–73. Reprinted in E. George Payne, ed. *Readings in Educational Sociology.* New York: Prentice-Hall, 1934.

Findlay, Joseph J. *Principles of Class Teaching.* London: Macmillan and Co., 1911.

Foght, Harold W. *The American Rural School.* New York: The Macmillan Company, 1912.
Foster, Harold H. *Principles of Teaching in Secondary Education.* New York: Charles Scribner's Sons, 1921.
Frasier, George W. and Winfred D. Armentrout. *An Introduction to Education.* Chicago: Scott, Foresman and Company, 1924.
Gesell, Arthur L. and Beatrice C. Gesell. *The Normal Child and Primary Education.* Boston: Ginn and Company, 1912.
Gilmour, R. "What Shall the Schools Teach?" *The Forum* VI (June 1888): 454–60.
Goddard, Henry H. "The Gifted Child." *The Journal of Educational Sociology* (February 1933): 354–61. Reprinted in E. George Payne, ed. *Readings in Educational Sociology.* New York: Prentice-Hall, 1934.
Good, Carter V., Arvil Barr, and Douglas Scates. *The Methodology of Educational Research.* New York: D. Appleton-Century Company, Inc., 1935.
Greenwood, James M. *Principles of Education Practically Applied to Schools.* New York: D. Appleton and Company, 1901.
Gregory, B. C. *Better Schools.* New York: The Macmillan Company, 1912
Hall, G. Stanley (and some of his pupils). "The Contents of Children's Minds." In G. Stanley Hall, ed. *Aspects of Child Life and Education.* Boston: Ginn and Company, 1907. Reprinted in Judith Krieger Gardner and Howard Gardner eds. *Classics in Child Development.* New York: Arno Press, 1975
Hall, John W. and Alice C. K. Hall. *The Question as a Factor in Teaching.* Boston: Houghton Mifflin Company, 1916.
Hanes, L. N. "Hygienic School Environment." *Educational Hygiene from the Pre-School Period to the University*, edited by Louis Rapeer, 312–29. New York: Charles Scribner's Sons 1915.
Hanus, Paul H. *A Modern School.* New York: The Macmillan Company, 1905.
Harris, William T. *The City School.* Syracuse, New York: C.W. Bardeen, Publisher, 1906.
———. *The Psychologic Foundations of Education.* New York: D. Appleton and Co., 1898. Reprinted in Lawrence Cremin, ed. *American Education: Its Men, Ideas, and Institutions.* New York: Arno Press, 1969.
Hart, Joseph K. *Educational Resources of Village and Rural Communities.* New York: The Macmillan Company, 1914.
Henderson, C. Hanford. *Education and the Larger Life.* Boston: Houghton Mifflin Company, 1902.
Henderson, Charles R. *Introduction to the Study of the Dependent, Defective, and Delinquent Classes and Their Social Treatment.* Boston: D. C. Heath & Co., 1901.
Hinsdale, Burke A. *The Art of Study: A Manual for Teachers and Students of the Science and the Art of Teaching.* New York: American Book Company, 1900
Holley, Charles E. *The Teacher's Technique.* New York: The Century Company, 1924.
Holmes, Arthur. *Backward Children.* Indianapolis: The Bobbs-Merrill Company: 1915.
Horne, Herman H. *Psychological Principles of Education.* London: The Macmillan Company, 1909.
Howland, George. *Practical Hints for the Teachers of Public Schools.* New York: D. Appleton and Company, 1899.
James, William. *Talks to Teachers on Psychology: And to Students on Some of Life's Ideals.* New York: Henry Holt and Company, 1910.
Johnson, Charles H. "The Junior High School." *Proceedings of the National Education Association* (1916): 145–51.
Johonnot, James. *Principles and Practice of Teaching.* New York: D. Appleton and Company, 1881.
Jones, Olive M. *Teaching Children to Study: The Group System Applied.* New York: The Macmillan Company, 1909.
Judd, Charles H. *The Evolution of a Democratic School System.* Boston: Houghton Mifflin Company, 1918.
———. *Introduction to the Scientific Study of Education.* Boston: Ginn and Company, 1918.

Keith, John A. *Elementary Education: Its Problems and Processes.* Chicago: Scott, Foresman & Company, 1905.
Kendall, Calvin N. and George Mirick. *How to Teach the Fundamental Subjects.* Boston: Houghton Mifflin Company, 1915.
King, Irving. *The High-School Age.* Indianapolis: The Bobbs-Merrill Company, 1914.
———. *Social Aspects of Education.* New York: The Macmillan Company, 1913.
King, Robert M. *School Interests and Duties.* New York: American Book Company, 1894.
Kirkpatrick, Edwin A. *Fundamentals of Child Study: A Discussion of Instincts and Other Factors in Human Development with Practical Applications.* New York: The Macmillan Company, 1916.
Kilpatrick, William H. *Source Book in the Philosophy of Education.* New York: The Macmillan Company, 1934.
Krug, Edward A. *The Shaping of the American High School: 1880–1920.* Madison: The University of Wisconsin Press, 1969.
Lewis, Ervin E. *Personnel Problems of the Teaching Staff.* New York: The Century Company 1925.
Lewis, W. D. "High School Administration." *Principles of Secondary Education,* edited by Paul Monroe, 174–232. New York: The Macmillan Company, 1914.
Livermore, Daniel P. "Women's Mental Status." *The Forum* V (March 1888): 90–98.
Long Jr., Edward K. *Introductory Psychology for Teachers.* Baltimore: Warwick & York, Inc. 1922.
McCord, Clinton P. Medical Supervision and the Exceptional Child." *Educational Hygiene from the Pre-School Period to the University,* edited by Louis Rapeer, 294–311. New York: Charles Scribner's Sons, 1915.
McEvoy, Thomas J. *The Science of Education.* Brooklyn: T. J. McEvoy, Publisher, 1911.
McKenny, Charles. *The Personality of the Teacher.* Chicago: Row, Peterson & Co., 1910.
McMurry, Charles A. *Conflicting Principles in Teaching and How to Adjust to Them.* Boston: Houghton Mifflin Company, 1914.
———. *The Elements of General Method Based on the Principles of Herbart.* Bloomington, Illinois: Public-School Publishing Company, 1895.
———. *Public School Methods, vol. 3.* Chicago: School Methods Company, 1912.
———. *Teaching by Projects: A Basis for Purposeful Study.* New York: The Macmillan Company, 1927.
MacVannel, John A. *The College Course in the Principles of Education.* Chicago: University of Chicago Press: Chicago, 1906.
Marsh, J. Frank. *The Teacher Outside the School.* Yonkers-on-Hudson, New York: World Book Company, 1928.
Maxwell, Charles R. *The Observation of Teaching.* Boston: Houghton Mifflin, 1917.
Maxwell, William H. "Examinations as Tests for Promotion. *Journal of Proceedings and Addresses of the National Education Association* (1890): 137.
Milner, Florence. *The Teacher.* New York: Scott, Foresman and Company, 1912.
Monroe, Paul. "Historic Sketch of Secondary Education." *Principles of Secondary Education,* edited by Paul Monroe, 16–70. New York: The Macmillan Company, 1914.
Monroe, Walter S. and Ruth Streitz. "*Directing Learning in the Elementary School.* Garden City, New Jersey: Doubleday, Doran & Company, Inc., 1932.
Morehouse, Frances M. "*The Discipline of the School.* Boston: D. C. Heath & Co., Publishers, 1914.
Morgan, John J. *The Psychology of the Unadjusted School Child.* New York: The Macmillan Company, 1930.
"Motion-Picture Schoolhouses to Prevent War," *Current Opinion* XLVI, no. 4 (April 1919): 234–35.
Myers, George E. "Moral Training in the School: A Comparative Study. *Pedagogical Seminary* XIII (December 1906): 409–60.
Neet, George W. *Studies in Pedagogy.* Valparaiso, Indiana: M. E. Bogarte, Publisher, 1903.
O'Shea, Michael V. *Everyday Problems of Teachers.* Indianapolis: The Bobbs-Merrill Company, 1912.

———. *Social Development and Education.* Boston: Houghton Mifflin Company, 1909.
Palmer, George H. *The Ideal Teacher.* Boston: Houghton Mifflin, 1908.
Parker, Franklin W. *Talks on Pedagogics.* New York: E. L. Kellogg & Co., 1894.
———. *Talks on Teaching.* New York: The A.S. Barnes Company, 1883.
Payne, E. George. "Narcotic Addiction as an Educational Problem." *Readings in Educational Sociology,* edited by E. George Payne, 121–26. New York: Prentice-Hall, 1934.
Payne, E. George and J. L. Archer. "Narcotics and Education." *The Journal of Educational Sociology* 4, no. 6 (February 1931): 370–79.
Payne, William H. *The Education of Teachers.* Richmond: B. F. Johnson Publishing, 1901.
Perry, Jr. Arthur C. *Discipline as a School Problem.* Boston: Houghton Mifflin Company, Boston. (1915).
———. *The Management of the City School.* New York: The Macmillan Company, 1908.
———. *The Status of the Teacher.* Boston: Houghton Mifflin Company, 1912.
Phelps, William L. *Teaching in School and College.* New York: The Macmillan Company, 1912.
Pitkin, Walter B. *The Art of Learning.* New York: McGraw-Hill, 1931.
Putnam, Daniel. *A Manual of Pedagogics.* New York: Silver, Burdett and Company, 1899.
Rice, Joseph M. *The Public School System of the United States.* New York: The Century Co. 1893. Reprinted in Lawrence Cremin, ed. *American Education: Its Men, Ideas, and Institutions.* New York: Arno Press, 1969.
———. *The Rational Spelling Book: Part One.* New York: American Book Company, 1898.
Rice, Martin P. "The Future of Radio Education." *The Journal of the National Education Association* XIII (March 1924): 82–83.
Roark, Ruric N. *Psychology in Education.* New York: American Book Company, 1895.
Salmon, David. *The Art of Teaching.* London: Longmans, Green, and Co., 1903.
Saunders, Randall N. *The Teacher and the Times.* Syracuse: C.W. Bardeen, 1911.
Search, Preston. *An Ideal School, or Looking Forward.* New York: D. Appleton and Company, 1902.
Seeley, Levi. *Elementary Pedagogy.* New York: Hinds, Noble & Eldredge, 1906.
———. *History of Education.* American Book Company, 1899.
Shaw, Edward R. *School Hygiene.* London: The Macmillan Company, 1910.
Smith, William H. *All the Children of All the People.* New York: The Macmillan Company, 1912.
Spencer, Herbert. *Education: Intellectual, Moral, and Physical.* New York: A. L. Burt, Publisher, 1860.
Stark, William E. *Every Teacher's Problems.* New York: American Book Company, 1922.
Stevenson, John A. *The Project Method of Teaching.* New York: The Macmillan Company, 1922.
Stormzand, Martin J. *Progressive Methods of Teaching.* Boston: Houghton Mifflin Company, 1924.
Strayer, George D. *A Brief Course in the Teaching Process.* New York: The Macmillan Company, 1911.
Strayer, George D. and N. L. Engelhardt. *The Classroom Teacher at Work in American Schools.* New York: American Book Company, 1920.
Strayer, George D. and Naomi Norsworthy. *How to Teach.* New York: The Macmillan Company, 1922.
Swift, Edgar J. *Learning and Doing.* Indianapolis, Indiana: Bobbs-Merrill Company, 1914.
Taylor, Joseph S. *Art of Class Management and Discipline.* New York: A. S. Barnes & Company, 1903.
Terman, Lewis M. *The Hygiene of the School Child.* Boston: Houghton Mifflin Company: 1914.
———. *The Measurement of Intelligence.* Boston: Houghton Mifflin Company, 1916.
Thorndike, Edward L. *Education: A First Book.* New York: The Macmillan Company, 1912. Reprinted in Howard Gardner and Judith Krieger Gardner, eds. *Classics in Psychology* New York: Arno Press, 1973.

Trabue, Marion R. *Measuring Results in Education.* New York: American Book Company, 1924.
Tyler, John M. *Growth and Education.* Boston: Houghton Mifflin Company, 1907.
U.S. Department of Commerce. "Statistical Abstract of the United States, 1937." www2.census.gov/prod2/statcomp/documents/1937-01.pdf(accessed December 20, 2010).
U.S. Department of Commerce. "Statistical Abstract of the United States, 1940." www2.census.gov/prod2/statcomp/documents/1940-01.pdf(accessed December 20, 2010).
Vanderwalker, Nina C. *The Kindergarten in American Education.* The Macmillan Company: New York, 1908. Reprinted in Lawrence Cremin, ed. *American Education: Its Men, Ideas, and Institutions.* New York: Arno Press, 1971.
Waldo, Frank. "The Educational Use of the Typewriter." *Education* XXII (April 1902): 484–92.
Waples, Douglas. *Problems in Classroom Method.* New York: The Macmillan Company, 1929.
Weeks, Ruth M. *The People's School: A Study in Vocational Training.* Boston: Houghton Mifflin Company, 1912.
Weimer, Hermann. *The Way to the Heart of the Pupil.* New York: The Macmillan Company: 1913.
White, Emerson E. *The Art of Teaching: A Manual.* New York: American Book Company: 1901.
———. *The Elements of Pedagogy.* New York: American Book Company, 1886.
———. *School Management.* New York: American Book Company: New York. 1893
Wile, Ira S. "Sex Hygiene and Sex Education." *Educational Hygiene from the Pre-School Period to the University,* edited by Louis Rapeer, 549–66. New York: Charles Scribner's Sons, 1915.
Wilson, H. B. and G. M.Wilson. *The Motivation of School Work.* Boston: Houghton Mifflin Company, 1921.
Wilson, Lewis A. "Organization and Administration of Special Education in the Public Schools." *The Journal of Educational Sociology* (February, 1933): 371–77. Reprinted in E. George Payne, ed. *Readings in Educational Sociology.* New York: Prentice-Hall, 1934.
Winship, Albert E. *Danger Signals for Teachers.* Chicago: Forbes & Company, 1919.
———. "Professional Sentiment." *Addresses and Proceedings of the National Education Association* (1899): 230.
Winslow, Hubbard. "The Dangerous Tendency to Innovations and Extremes in Education. *Proceedings of the American Institute of Instruction* (1834): 169–79.
Woodard, James W. "Education as a Social Problem." *The Journal of Educational Sociology* (January 1933): 290–304. Reprinted in E. George Payne, ed. *Readings in Educational Sociology.* New York: Prentice-Hall, 1934.
Woodley, O. I. and M. V. Woodley. *The Profession of Teaching.* Boston: Houghton Mifflin Company, 1917.

Index

ability, 75
acquisition of knowledge, 76
adult models, 76
administrators, 1, 2
Almack, John C., 92, 97, 123, 142
Archer, J. L., 22
Armentrout, Winfred D., 61, 101, 103, 114, 145
Arnold, Felix, 34, 75
Arnold, Sarah L., 15, 28, 143, 144, 149
athletic misconduct, 14
attention and inattention, 85; and interest, 87, 88, 89; securing, 38; span of children, 86
attitudes of children, 14; of teachers, 143
authority, 14
autocratic control of teachers, 2
Ayres, C. E., 101
Ayres, Leonard P., 41, 60, 79

Bagley, William Chandler, 2, 16, 17, 18, 25, 29, 45, 51, 79, 88, 99, 104, 107, 109, 111, 128, 133, 142, 146, 154
Bain, Alexander, xvi, 145
Barr, Arvil S., 62, 130, 148
behavioral objectives, 27
Bennett, Henry E., 36
Benson, Arthur F., 104
Betts, George H., 17, 29, 38, 50, 51, 88, 99, 100, 103, 110, 127, 134
blame for poor school work, 97

boards of education, 2
Bobbitt, J. Franklin, 27, 44, 50, 53, 59, 120, 121
Bonser, Frederick G., 83, 122
Book, William F., 138
Boone, Richard, 108
boredom, 86
Bowden, A. O., 62
Boyer, Charles C., 14, 82, 83, 118, 121, 146, 152
brain-based learning, 76
brain fatigue, 77
Briggs, Thomas H., 30, 46, 98, 111, 122
Brooks, Eugene C., 2, 5, 40, 136, 140
Burke, Frederick, 10
Burton, William, 130
busy work, xvii, 28
Butler, Nicholas M., 58, 63

Caldwell, Otis W., 32, 160
Cary, Edward, 51
Chapman, J. Crosby, 101, 128
Charters, W. W., 18, 31, 34, 37, 51, 52, 81, 153
child with initiative, 9
children, 7, 8; at school and at home, 15; backward, 69; maladjusted, 10; misfit, 10; nervous, 10; peculiar, 11; quiet, 11; of today, 9
child-study movement, 8
chloroform, 22

Clark, S. H., 123
class size, 97
classroom management, 13, 15, 16, 17, 164
classroom practices, 27
classroom routines, 28
classroom tone, 46
classroom size, 98
Coe, George, 26
Coffman, Lotus D., 122
cognitive field theory, 77
college entrance exams, 98, 157
Colvin, Stephen S., 79, 88, 99
Comenius, 81
communication among grade levels, 98
constructivism, xvii, 77
Corson, Oscar T., 55, 94, 106, 137
Counts, George S., 60, 66, 101, 128, 161
Courtis, Stuart A., 160
cramming, 78
Crawford, Claude C., 89
credit for home activities, 49
critical thinking, 28
Cubberley, Elwood P., xvi, 1, 4, 5, 35, 55, 59, 64, 92, 135
cultivation of the intellect, 28
curriculum, 49, 50, 164; change, 50, 51; development, 51; expansion, 51, 52; influence of colleges on, 53; response, 52; socializing, 54

Davenport, Eugene, xiv, 55
Davis, Sheldon E., 6, 19, 32, 37, 41, 52, 113, 127, 130, 141, 147, 148, 152, 153
Davidson, Thomas, 140
Dearborn, Ned H., 28, 72, 92, 111, 125, 128
DeGarmo, Charles, xiv, 21, 57, 66, 111
demand for good teachers, 135
democracy in education, xiii, xiv, xv, 57
deportment, 19
determining success in the classroom, 78
detriments to higher order thinking skills, 78
developing cooperation and interest, 86
Dewey, Evelyn, 21, 60, 76, 80
Dewey, John, xiv, 3, 7, 8, 21, 43, 44, 47, 58, 59, 60, 63, 74, 76, 80, 88, 111, 128, 158

discipline, 19, 20, 21; through knowledge, 21
disobedience, 21
distance education, 135
Dr. Spankster's tonic, 17
don't smile until Christmas, 22
Draper, Andrew S., 149
dropouts, 113, 114
drugs, 22
Dutton, Samuel T., 24

Earhart, Lida B., 35, 42, 54
early schoolmaster, 135
easy entry to the teaching profession, 127, 128
Edison, Thomas, 133, 139
education, 57; definitions of, 58, 59; faith in, 60; federal role, 61; feminization of, 61; history of, 62; more vs. better, 53; purpose of, 64; religion in, 65; relevance of, 54, 112; the study of, 65, 66
education for girls, 99, 100
education literature, rise of, vi, xv, xvi
education as opposed to schooling, 60
educational decision making, 60
educational panaceas, 60
effects of failure, 79
elementary schools, 100, 101
Ellis, William J., 72
encouragement in the classroom, 87
Engelhardt, N. L., 6, 46, 51, 62, 82, 102, 122, 130
English teachers, 136
Essentialism, 163
Examinations, school, 159
exceptional children, 30, 69, 70, 165
experiential education, 53

fatigue, 79
Faunce, William H. P., 9
Findlay, Joseph J., 23, 30, 31, 47
fires in schools, 108
first day of school, 29
flash cards, 29
Foght, Harold W., 134
Foster, Harold H., 31, 43, 78, 106, 151
Frasier, George W., 61, 101, 103, 114, 145
funding for schools, 108, 109

Gesell, Arthur L., 7, 8, 21, 85, 108
Gesell, Beatrice C., 7, 8, 21, 85, 108
gifted education 70
Gilmour, R., 65
Goddard, Henry H., 70
Good, Carter V., 62
grade levels, 102
Greenwood, James M., 24
Gregory, B. C., 14, 119
grouping, 29, 30

Hall, Alice C. K., 9, 44
Hall, G. Stanley, 7, 17, 80
Hall, John W., 9, 44
Hall, Otis E., 17, 29, 38, 51, 88, 110, 127, 134
Hanes, L. N., 96, 103
Hanus, Paul H., xvii, 98, 131
happiness as a school goal, 102
Harris, William T., xvi, 20, 78
Hart, Joseph K., 115
Henderson, C. Hanford, 110
Henderson, Charles R., 71, 72, 73, 71
heredity the effects of, 70
heroin, 22
heuristic method, 151
high expectations, 30, 31
high schools, 97, 103; enrollments 1890–1935, xiv
high standards, 31
Hinsdale, Burke A., 76
Holley, Charles E., 21, 52, 74
Holmes, Arthur, 69, 70, 72, 82, 159
home conditions, influence of, 92
homework, 31, 32
Horne, Herman H., 22, 38, 45, 77, 139, 147
Howland, George, 3, 23, 24, 26, 34, 39, 41, 83
humor, 21, 32
hypnotism, 22

ideal instruction, 152
I have gone home, 80
imagination, 33, 30
immigration education, 62
independent thinking, 33
individualized instruction, 34
in loco parentis, 93
initiative, 34

innovations, 152
in-service education, 128
instruction driven by tests, 158
intellectual blinders, 158
intelligence testing, 158
introducing new material, 152, 153

James, William, 20, 89
Jewell, Frederick, 14
Johnson, Charles H., 104
Johonnot, James, xvi, 119, 153
Jones, Olive M., 29, 60
Judd, Charles H., xviii, 17, 30, 34, 40, 50, 49, 94, 100, 110, 114, 154
junior high school, 104

Keith, John A., 20, 24, 38, 45, 58, 83, 104, 107, 109, 142
Kendall, Calvin N., 35, 136, 147
kindergarten, vi, 95, 102, 105
King, Irving, 32, 54, 108, 113
King, Robert M., 19, 93
Kirkpatrick, Edwin A., 22
Krug, Edward A., xiv

Lang, Albert, 92, 97, 123, 142
lateral entry teachers, 130
learning, 75, 80, 81; by doing, 81; curves, 81; styles, 81, 82
learning from teaching, 153
lesson plans, 34, 35, 164
Lewis, Ervin E., 1, 5, 129
Lewis, W. D., 97
lifelong learners, 82
Livermore, Daniel P., 99
Long, Edward K. Jr., 29, 81

Machiavelli, Niccolo, xix
MacVannel, John A., 66
maintaining order, 23
Marsh, J. Frank, 32, 142, 159
Maxwell, Charles R., 129, 148
Maxwell, William H., 159
McCord, Clinton P., 69, 70, 71
McEvoy, Thomas J., 79, 97
McKenny, Charles, 41, 45, 46, 101, 106, 138
McMurry, Charles A., 112, 120, 123, 147
me generation, 114

memory, 83
mentors for new teachers, 129
micromanagement, 3
Milner, Florence, 20, 94, 134, 137
Mirick, George, 35, 124, 136, 147
Monroe, Paul, 103
Monroe, Walter S., 122
moral education, 53
Morehouse, Frances M., 22, 45, 86, 107, 114, 148
Morgan, John J., 10, 11, 24, 34, 42, 59, 124
motion-picture schoolhouses, 139
motivation of students, 85, 89
multicultural education, 63
Myers, George E., 30

need to know as the basis of learning, 83
Neet, George W., 127, 130
National Education Association, 63, 112
new education, 63
Norsworthy, Naomi, 33, 39, 46, 80, 89
Nutt, H. W., 89

office referrals, 23
open air schools, 8, 106
O'Shea, Michael V., 14, 16, 17, 21, 54, 80, 100

Palmer, George H., 89, 144, 146
parents, 91, 93, 94; angry, 91, 92; attitudes, 93; expectations for teachers, 93; going downtown to report the teacher, 91; skills, 93
Parker, Francis W., xvii, 33, 58, 86, 105, 117, 118, 119, 120, 135, 141, 157, 158, 159
Payne, E. George, 22, 118
Payne, William H., 43, 58, 102, 125, 146, 145, 152, 154
Perry, Arthur C. Jr., 3, 4, 15, 17, 18, 19, 37, 91, 93, 94, 137, 145
Pickard, J. L., 23, 26, 93, 141
Phelps, William L., 25
philosophy of education, the need for, 140
Pitkin, Walter B., 82
political influence of teachers, 140
posture, 35, 36, 125
poverty, the effects of, 114
preaching, 20, 36

pride in American education, 64
principals, 3, 4; chief duty of, 3
Progressive education, 50, 163; weakness of, 66
project method, 36
punishment, 23, 37; corporal punishment, 17, 18, 25
Putnam, Daniel, 23, 51, 53, 77, 81, 139, 152, 153

Quackenbos, Dr., 22
questions, 37; taxonomy of, 43

racial differences in education, 115
Rapeer, Louis W., 108
reading, 123
reading aloud, 37
recess, 107
regimentation of schooling, 64
research departments, 107
resistance to change among teachers, 141; among parents, 94
respect for social and ethical law, 115
responsibility, 24
retarded children, 71
rewards for good teaching, 142
Rice, Joseph M., 46, 63, 95, 96, 117, 124
Rice, Martin P., 135
rights of special education children, 71
Riverside education series, xvi
Roark, Ruric N., 19, 43, 76, 146

Salmon, David, 28, 36
Saunders, Randall N., 9, 18, 31, 125
Scates, Douglas, 62
school as a learning community, 108
school enrollments, growth of, xiv, 95
school failure, 108
school janitor, 103
school wagon driver, 110
school reform, xiii, xiv, xviii, xix, 110, 164
school work, 37; fundamental difficulty with, 87
schools, 95, 96; antiquated, 96; better, 96; critics, 99; as factories, 101; fatal defect of, 101; overburdened, 106; pleasant, 106; size, 110
scientific management of schools, 4
scolding, 24

Scott, Harriet, xvii, 77
Search, Preston, 31, 33, 39, 53, 102, 107, 112, 121
seating of students, 38
Seeley, Levi, 2, 43, 62
self control, 24, 25
self development, 38
self fulfilling prophecy, 38
Shaw, Edward R., 31
Silko, Leslie, xiii
single sex classrooms, 111
skipping grades, 39
slow children, 71, 122
Smith, William H., 113, 154
Social Efficiency Movement, 163
social life of teachers, 142
social promotion of students, 39, 40
socialism, 65
soup kitchen theory of education, 88
special education, 69, 72, 73
special education instruction, 73
Spencer, Herbert, 19, 38, 43, 65, 67, 93
standard course of study, 55
Starch, Daniel, 124
Stark, William E., 131, 140
Stevenson, John A., 36
Stormzand, Martin J., 81
Strayer, George D., 6, 33, 39, 46, 51, 62, 80, 82, 89, 102, 122, 130, 138
Streitz, Ruth, 122
student desks, 111, 125
students, 113, 4; discussions with, 41; individual differences, 33, 34; promotion of, 41
stupid pupils, 10, 74, 141
subject matter, 117, 125, 51, 52; arithmetic, 32, 118; composition, 118; drug education, 118; geography, 119; grammar, 119, 120; language, 101, 120; literature, 120; mathematics, 120, 121; phonics and whole language, 121, 122; physical education, 122; reading, 101, 123; science, 123; sex education, 123, 124; spelling, 124; teacher knowledge of, 144; temperance, 125
substitute teaching, 142
success the effects of in the classroom, 41, 42

superintendents advice to principals, 4, 5; turnover, 5
supervision of children, 13, 25; of teachers, 5, 6
support for teachers, 143
Swift, Edgar J., 37, 42, 58, 80, 83, 136

taking children as they are, 42
taking notes, 42
tardiness, 25
Taylor, Joseph S., 16, 17, 25, 87
taxonomy of objectives for thinking, 83
teacher health, 138
teacher preparation, 127, 129; as educational leadership, 128
teacher sense of humor, 21
teacher shortage, 129
teacher talk, 43
teacher turnover, 145, 146
teachers, 133, 146, 147; beginning, 134; born, 134; forgotten, 136; of the future, 144; general as the, 136; high school, 138; ideal, 138; mediator, 139; mood, 144; reflective, 141; as role model, 139; scholarship, 144, 145; status, 145; stress, 142; temperament, 145; wise, 149
teachers' meetings, 130
teachers need to get a life, 137
teaching, 43, 44; as leadership, 45; and learning, 44; measuring results, 159; theory into practice, 147
teaching as patriotic work, 140
teaching methods, 151, 153, 154, 165
teaching vs. telling, 152, 155
Terman, Lewis M., 10, 32, 33, 39, 57, 65, 70, 158
tests and testing, 157, 158, 160, 161, 165
textbooks, xvi, 1, 45, 46, 119, 154
Thorndike, Edward L., 58, 61, 102, 109, 113, 115, 144, 155
time on task, 46, 124
Trabue, Marion R., 64
Tyler, John M., 53, 97, 105, 157
types of learners, 46
types of teachers who fail, 147, 148
typewriters, 125

unhealthy classrooms, 112

universal education, xiv, 66
untrained teachers, 130, 131

value of education books, 131
Vanderwalker, Nina C., 7, 105

wait time, 47
Waldo, Frank, 125
Waples, Douglas, 28, 86, 134
WCTU. *See* Women's Christian Temperance Union
weakness of progressive education, 66
Weeks, Ruth M., 88, 112
Weimer, Hermann, 114
what ails youth, 26
what knowledge is of most worth?, 67
whipping post, xvii, 26

White, Emerson E., xvii, 19, 28, 78, 103, 121, 146, 160
Wile, Ira S., 123
Wilson, H. B., xv, 4, 67, 87, 89, 120
Wilson, G. M., xv, 4, 67, 87, 89, 120
Wilson, Lewis A., 73
Winship, Albert E., 6, 44, 129, 143, 144
Winslow, Hubbard, 152
with-it-ness, 47
Women's Christian Temperance Union (WCTU), 125
Woodard, James W., 64
Woodley, M. V., 59, 106, 143, 160
Woodley, O. I., 59, 106, 143, 160
work force in America, 112
working conditions of teachers, 149

About the Author

Corey R. Lock is professor of educational leadership at the University of North Carolina–Charlotte.

www.ingramcontent.com/pod-product-compliance
Lightning Source LLC
Chambersburg PA
CBHW061832300426
44115CB00013B/2350